The Chinese

Text by
J.-B. Grosier

Crescent Books
New York

Crédits : B.N./Estampes : 14b, 15, 19, 20, 33b, 35, 37a, b, 70, 71, 82, 89a, b, 93a — Bulloz : 42, 53b, 55b, 88, 90b, 96 — Doumic/Atlas : 94 — Dulevant/Gemini : 40, 52b, 54a — Giraudon : 1, 10, 48a, 49a, 50, 54b, 55a, 78 — Goldner/Atlas : 66, 68a — Horold/Vloo : 68b — Keystone : 76, 77 — Lauros/Giraudon : 11, 22a, b, 23, 39b, c, 52a, 80, 81, 86a — Mandel/Gemini : 4, 12a, b, 17, 30, 39a, 44, 45, 47, 53d, 85, 91, 93b, 95a — Marzari/Gemini : 56, 86b — Migot/Atlas : 79 — Pavard/Vloo : 5a — Pavard/Fotogram : 72a, b — Pell/Atlas : 69a — Spaak/Fotogtam : 73b — Viollet : 2, 7, 8, 29b, 57, 62, 63, 64, 65b, 73a, 74a, b, c, 75, 90a, 95b.

For long centuries since the most ancient times, and until the dawn of our twentieth century, China has maintained a great consistency in many different spheres; so in the present book we are concerned with a civilization well over a thousand years old. Though modern China is not discussed in the following pages, quite certainly one can only properly appreciate its present situation by finding out about its past which is, in any case, of great importance in itself.

1

For several centuries the people of China were divided into seven grades: mandarins, warriers, scholars, bonzes, peasants, labourers and merchants.

Full mandarins, with robe and sword, almost always came from the last three grades of citizen, so when a child seemed promising his parents would push him to study in order to fulfil their ambition for him to become a mandarin. Then his years of study and knowledge gained would be repaid by the achievement of this high position

Left: the stone portico of the famous Avenue of the Mings, near Peking (1540). Above: an emperor of ancient times, on horseback.

which, however, he could only take up in a different region from the one where he was brought up.

For those people who took up the career of warrier it was unlikely that they would ever achieve the status of superior officer or commander. Even when they did reach a high rank after years of strenuous drill and great determination, this did not mean that they could then accumulate great riches, because they spent most of their money on equipment which had to be as spectacular as possible; the money they had left was spent on the comforts of life which they much enjoyed, and in addition they were obliged to make long and costly journeys from one end of the empire to the other.

The scholars were men who aspired to a literary career or to public office, or philo-

3

sophers engaged on reading and interpreting the ancient texts, or former mandarins who had retired and frequently were destitute. There was always a fixed number of scholars: enough to fill the various occupations the State had set aside for them.

The bonzes, tao-tses and lamas were the ministers of the three religious sects in China. There were a great many of them, but though they lived outside State control and were disapproved of by the law, they still managed to acquire considerable riches which they possessed in common. Without doubt they constituted the most opulent class in the country.

The peasant class was made up of the largest portion of the population and their useful occupation was highly regarded by the government which upheld their rights more energetically than those of any other group.

The labourers did not have to pay any taxes, but there were so many of them that they had to be in constant competition with each other in order to obtain any success at all.

As for the merchants, they were divided into four categories: those who concentrated on foreign trade, those who concerned themselves with the import and export of merchandise from one end of the empire to the other, those who kept warehouses and sold their goods wholesale and finally the merchants who sold retail goods. On the whole, one can estimate that the first three categories of merchants could accumulate a larger fortune than the other six grades of citizens.

The government of China was almost wholly concerned with internal affairs. This vast empire had very few relations even with its closest neighbours. The Chinese always preferred to concentrate on improving their own resources and had no interest at all in opening up their frontiers to foreign peoples.

The great antiquity of this empire is evident in the order and stability of its establishments which have grown up over the centuries. Especially in matters of policy and administration, there were never any sudden changes or rapid completions, and for over two thousand years there could be found here institutions which were clearly the result of long years of experience and development.

Throughout their history they followed the custom of carrying out annually a census of the population in the empire and people were counted in each family, district and province. This gave a general picture of all individuals without distinction of age, sex or social status. Moreover, they also made a second detailed census, this time only of the lower orders from the age of sixteen to fifty. This served to determine the orders of duty, to assist general enquiries and to facilitate the work of the police, among other things.

Agriculture was the main concern of the people who regarded it as the first and most noble of occupations, because it served the primary needs of society. It naturally followed that those who worked the land were the object of the highest consideration. To provoke, oppress or even to fail to help them at the proper time were crimes for which not even the mandarins were pardoned.

From left to right: 8th century ceramic; one of the statues of the Avenue of the Mings, depicting a statue; two intellectuals chatting.

Throughout Chinese history one can find a particular type of man called a eunuch, who has played an important part in public affairs and has even been the author of some revolutions in that country.

Public records mention the existence of eunuchs from the time of Yao who died in the years 2258 B.C., and they specify that this degradation of a man was first of all inflicted as a punishment for some crime. This type of mutilation was the fourth of the tortures used at that time and was usually a punishment for slander, treachery or lewd behaviour.

The humiliating circumstances under which these eunuchs lived, continued for several centuries, but it was by means of an intrigue that at last their lot was improved. This happened in the reign of Emperor Yeou-ouan who acceded to the throne in the year 781 before Christ; one of his concubines, the notorious Pao-tze who is described in public records as being "the scourge of the Empire", used the help of a eunuch to stage a plot to force the emperor to repudiate his wife the empress and put her on the throne instead. When she did succeed in her aim and rose to power, she repaid the eunuch by giving him the most important job in the palace and gave prestigeous jobs to the other eunuchs too. From then on their condition was a far more satisfactory one.

By the time the Christian era began, that is under the Hane dynasty, the eunuch's lot ceased to be such a torture. Their prestige and authority became so great that this mutilation came to be regarded as a desirable means by which to reach a high position, and several voluntarily chose this method to attain their ambition.

Landscapes from the enormous expanse of China. Above: detail of an early painting; below: view of a gulf, from a print; right: lake at Nanking. Following pages: the Fu-Chun River (Hang Chou province).

2

The laws of ancient China almost all derive from the ethics laid down in the canonical books.

Thus all mandarins, whether governors of provinces or towns, had a duty to teach the law to the people who would gather around them twice a month for this purpose.

Article I. — Every man should most carefully carry out all the duties required by filial piety and in accordance with the deference owed by the younger brother to the elder.

Article II. — One should always hold the family ancestors in the greatest respect.

Article III. — In order that unity and peace should reign in the villages, quarrels and legal actions should be avoided as far as possible.

Article IV. — Those who follow the occupations of agricultural labourer or breeder of silkworms are worthy of high public esteem.

Article V. — Frugality, temperance, modesty, and an economy that is not miserly, should be the objects of meditation and a rule of conduct.

Article VI. — Care should be given to the efficient running of the public schools.

Article VII. — Each person should occupy himself with the duties for which his position makes him responsible.

Article VIII. — All private cliques or sects should be eradicated the moment they begin to form.

Article IX. — The people should often be reminded of the penal laws which have been laid down by sovereign authority. Those who are coarse and intractable can only be controlled by fear.

Article X. — The rules of courtesy should be carefully studied and observed.

Article XI. — One should apply oneself to taking good care of one's children and younger brothers.

Article XII. — One should abstain from all slanderous accusations.

Article XIII. — To harbour any criminal who has been condemned to lead a vagrant and solitary life for his crimes, is tantamount to being their accomplice.

Article XIV. — All taxes exacted by the sovereign should be paid exactly and punctually, to avoid the vexation of enquiries and demands being made.

Left: an emperor in ancient times visiting one of the provinces (plate taken from the "Historical Collection of the Lives of the Emperors of China", an early manuscript now in the Bibliothèque Nationale, Paris). Above: bronze plaque from Inner Mongolia.

Article XV. — People should collaborate with the heads of their district who have been appointed in each town. This is the best method by which to prevent larceny and bring ill-doers to justice.

Article XVI. — Outbursts of anger should be kept under control to avoid greater dangers ensuing.

There were a great number of laws concerning marriage. A man could only have one legitimate wife and she had to be of the same social class and approximately the same age as himself. But he could keep several concubines who were permitted to enter his house without any formalities being necessary.

These second-class wives were totally dependent on the legitimate wife, they had to obey and wait upon her, and their children belonged to her. These children were only allowed to regard her as their mother, and if she should die they had to wear mourning for three years during which time they were not allowed to study for examinations nor abandon their duties. No such sacrifices were required of them when their natural mother died.

A widow or a widower were quite free to remarry if they so desired. In this case equality of social status was no longer a prime necessity and a widower could even choose his new wife from among his concubines; in any case this second marriage required very few formalities.

If after having had children a woman was then widowed, she became entirely free to do as she liked; her family had no power either to force her to marry or not to marry again, unless she agreed to it by her own free will.

Widows who were poor and had no male heirs, however, could not enjoy any such privileges. In this case the parents-in-law could find another husband for them without even asking their opinion in advance.

Divorce was permitted in China, as in all other countries in ancient times, but it was

Above : the workings of justice depicted on a Cantonese lacquer portiere. Right, the seals of a chancellor.

not so easily obtained. There were seven grounds for divorce, as follows: 1. Habitual and absolute disobedience. 2. Sterility. 3. Adultery. 4. Jealousy: this means excessive jealousy which may lead the legitimate wife to prevent her husband from taking another woman, to whom he is entitled, so that a scandal is caused by her attitude. 5. An illness which provokes disgust, such as leprosy and epilepsy. 6. Malicious gossip. This is not so surprising as grounds for divorce when one realizes that the meaning here is not a condemnation of a constant flow of words in the ordinary sense, but rather of that dangerous chatter in a group of women who, by telling each other false rumours, malicious secrets or misleadingly treacherous confidences, cause trouble in the home and disunion in the family. 7. Theft: this was only grounds for divorce when the wife stole from her husband in order to enrich her own family.

This is the basic law on divorce in China, but it was subject to three exceptions. The first was that if the father, mother and elder brother of the wife were all dead, she could no longer be sent away from her husband's home because, as the law said, "*there had been a place from where this woman had been taken, but if this place no longer exists, then she can no longer be returned there*". The second case was that no divorce could take place when the parents-in-law were dead and the daughter-in-law had been in mourning for them for three years. Thirdly, if the husband had been poor at the time of his marriage and had then become rich, he could no longer divorce his wife; for as she had supported him and shared in his poverty during those early days, it would be unjust to send her away just at the time when abundance and comfort reigned in the home.

If a legitimate wife should furtively run away from her husband's house, he could take the matter to court and obtain a judgement authorizing him to sell the fugitive who had by this act ceased to be his wife and was now his slave. If she married another man after having run away, she was then strangled.

However, the law did come in aid of a woman who was abandoned by her husband. If he had been absent for three years, she

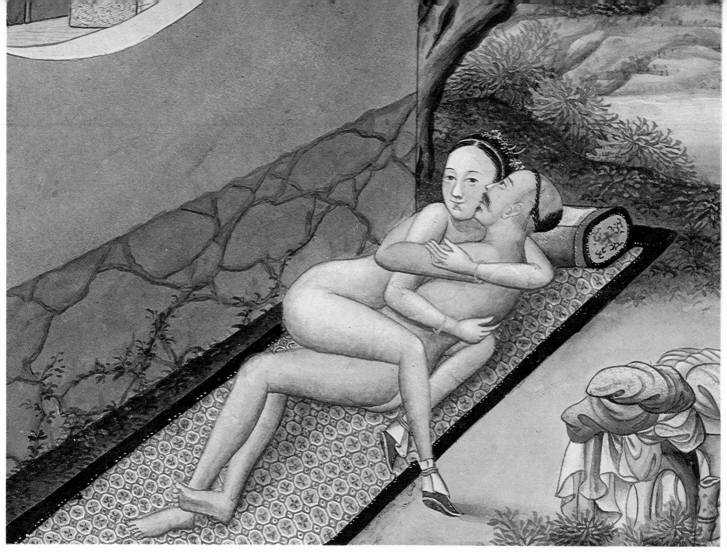

could present her case to the mandarins who would then authorize her to take another husband.

In certain circumstances the law could forbid a marriage or declare it nul and void if it had been contracted in defiance of its provisions. Here are some examples of cases when marriage could not take place:

1. If a young girl had been promised to a man and the presents had been sent to and accepted by their respective families, she could no longer marry any other man.

2. If the bridegroom's intermediary was shown a very beautiful girl, but a plain one turned up at the marriage ceremony, the marriage would then be cancelled. In addition, the daughter of a free man was not allowed to marry a slave.

3. A mandarin was never allowed to marry anyone from the province or city of which he was governor.

4. No Chinaman was allowed to marry while in mourning for either a father or a mother. If marriage promises had been made before

such a death, all preparations for the marriage had to be suspended.

5. Two brothers were not permitted to marry two sisters; a widower could not allow his son to marry the daughter of his second wife, and no two people who were related in any way, could ever marry.

Another law stipulated that a father was always responsible for the conduct of his children and even of his servants. Therefore he was charged with any misdeeds of theirs which he could have prevented.

A mother was not even allowed to make a will.

Since, according to the law, a son should not have more power over himself than his own father does, and any man's son was entitled to sell himself as a slave if he so desired, so it naturally followed that a father could sell his own son to slavery.

A man was considered a minor for as long as his father was alive.

When both parents had died, the eldest son took over all paternal duties towards his brothers and sisters who now owed him the same deference, obedience and respect as if he were their true father.

Top left : intimate scene, from a collection of erotic engravings. Left : emperor surrounded by men of letters. The caption reads: "Emperor Kouang-Ou, each evening after the day's business was concluded, used to summon the notables and the men of letters. He used to read with them the classical books of the law until well into the night". Above : Emperor Yao (in 2357 BC!). At the door of his palace he placed a tablet on which his subjects could write down their opinions about the progress of the empire; they banged a drum to alert the monarch.

Any person accused of a crime was sent to be judged by five to six courts, each of which would re-examine the case. Evidence was heard not only against the accused but also against the plaintiff and the witnesses, a procedure that was unique to China.

The accused was kept in prison till the trial had ended, but these prisons were not at all the dark and horrible places they are in so many other countries; on the contrary, they were spacious, clean and even fairly comfortable. A mandarin was instructed to pay frequent visits to the prisoners and he executed his duties towards them with enormous care, especially when one of them was ill, in which case he would call a doctor and personally supervise their treatment.

The seriousness of the crime determined the grade of punishment, of which the mildest was beating with a stick. This was regarded as merely a paternal from of correction and was not a dishonourable one. Even the Emperor would sometimes have one of his courtesans beaten, but afterwards he would receive her and be as pleasant to her as before. The number of strokes given to a person would be dependent on the gravity of the misdeed, though twenty was the minimum.

This stick, or *pan-tze,* was made of bamboo, a little flattened and enlarged at the base and polished towards the tip so that it could be used efficiently. Any mandarin could inflict this punishment as part of his duties.

Another punishment in China was the fixing of a yoke round a person's neck, which he carried with him everywhere he went. This yoke consisted of two pieces of wood, each one semi-circular, so that when they were joined together they would just fit round the neck, resting on his shoulders and so wide that he could not look down or bring his hands to his mouth. He could only eat when fed by someone, and had to carry this burden day and night. Its weight was graded according to the gravity of the crime.

This instrument of torture was usually worn for three months by those found guilty of theft, disturbance of public order or the tranquillity of a family, professional gambling, and so on.

The administration of several slaps on the face was a not uncommon punishment for missionaries and Christian Chinese.

Several crimes were punished by banishment, which was often for life, or by having to pull the royal barges for three years. A criminal could also have his cheeks branded by a red-hot iron; the resulting mark indicated the nature of the crime so that people would always know what he had done.

Armed robbery was punished with the death penalty. Pick-pockets, on the other hand, were branded on their left arm for the first offence, on their right arm for a second offence, but if caught a third time they were brought up before the criminal courts.

Any person found guilty of stealing from a member of his family was more severely punished than if he had stolen from an outsider.

Those found guilty of informing on their parents, grandparents, uncle or elder brother were condemned to one hundred strokes of the pan-tze and three years of exile if the information they gave proved to be true. If, however, it was false, then they were strangled.

Any girl who did not dutifully serve her parents and grandparents was condemned to one hundred strokes of the pan-tze; if she was insulting towards them she was strangled and if she wounded them she was tortured and then cut up into pieces.

When a younger brother used insulting words to his elder brother, the law condemned him to one hundred strokes of the pan-tze. He was condemned to exile if he raised his hand to him.

The burial ground for each family was sacred, untransferable and could not be seized by third parties. It was forbidden, under pain of death, to cut the trees till they had died of their own accord and a mandarin had been called in to establish their age.

Homicide received the death penalty. Anyone who killed his adversary during any kind of quarrel was strangled without

Statuette of the first Tsing emperor; he was deified. (Parma, China Museum).

possibility of remission.

The most shameful of all punishments was decapitation. This was reserved for murderers of the most wilful kind and other crimes of the same gravity.

Crimes against the state and high treason against the emperor brought the whole legal machine to bear upon the culprit without any possibility of mercy.

Any crime against the state brought the courts into instant action. The gathering of information and interrogations were followed by the most cruel tortures and usually the accused were executed the same day or the day after. Though justice in China could be considered as slow-moving, moderate, even rather indulgent for the less serious crimes, it became swift, bold and inexorable in its condemnation of any attack against the person of the sovereign or government officials.

There was a form of torture called *kiao* which consisted in being cut up into *ten thousand pieces* and was inflicted on those found guilty of crimes against the emperor, conspiracy against the state or open rebellion. This punishment existed only in China, where it remained in use for a long time. The criminal was tied to a stake, then the executioner drew a knife round the lower part of the skull and jawbones, detached the skin and drew it back over the eyes. After which he cut off various small pieces from the body and continued till too exhausted to wield his axe any more. Finally the remainder of the body was abandoned to the savagery of the crowd which finished off the cruel work.

A great many emperors had this torture carried out in its entirety, while others lessened some of its ferocity. The law, however, did not insist that every detail of the procedure be followed. It ordained punishment, and then the criminal could be disembowelled, cut to pieces and thrown in a river or into the ditch which served as a communal grave for all criminals.

People accused of a crime were considered innocent till they were actually proved guilty and condemned. Till that moment they could enjoy any comforts that were available to render the situation bearable, and if they were found innocent every help would be given

to them on their release.

It was permitted that any close relative of the guilty party could take his place to receive the punishment ordained by law, if the punishment was not a severe one and the guilty man was older than the relative. For example there was once a young man whose father had been condemned to be beaten. This young man clung to his father and begged to be punished in his place, so that the mandarin was so touched at this show of filial devotion that he pardoned the old man. Love of one's parents was so highly regarded in China that history supplies a great many accounts of this kind.

Soldiers were usually chosen to act as executioners, but there was nothing shameful about this duty and they were even proud of the strength and skill they brought to it. In Peking the executioner would accompany his victim to the torture chamber.

It is difficult for a Westerner to fully appreciate how little the Chinese value life; suicide is an everyday occurrence and is most frequently resorted to as an answer to failed ambition, jealousy, hate and vengeance.

China has been much criticised for the existence of infanticide in their society. However, this crime has never been as common as sometimes thought and usually only occurred in huge overcrowded cities and among those people whose way of life forced them to live in boats. The reason for it was always extreme poverty.

Above: extract from a silk roll (45 feet long and 2 1/2 feet high) on the theme of the tours of inspection of Emperor K'ang-Hi in the south of the country. The crowd awaits the emperor with deep reverence.
Left: street scene. Following pages: another scene from the travels of K'ang-Hi for purposes of inspection: the emperor's general staff.

3

The Chinese way of life is unlike that of any other known people, and this way of life has continued unchanged for centuries. Even now, in the middle of the 19th century, the Chinese continue as they have lived for four thousand years, their lives as isolated as in the past millennia, their beliefs and their actions unvaried.

If the Chinese have adhered so consistently to their own way of life, it is because it is so carefully safeguarded. Marriage, a condition looked upon favourably and encouraged by all the great legislators, receives special protection in China. Rarely indeed does it give rise to those scandals that are attendant upon marriage in so many other countries, making it a state in many cases more to be feared than sought after. Chinese law lays down terrible penalties for anyone coming between a couple: the death penalty is common for the seduction either of a wife or of a daughter.

In China, women are virtually prisoners in their own homes. A Chinese man marries

Right : reduced models of a fortified farm (Han period), a private house, and a tower. Above : carillon of an aristocrat.

without having even set eyes upon the woman who is to be his bride. To build up a picture of her looks, her figure, her character he must rely upon the reports of a female relation or some other woman acting as a go-between. Nonetheless, if he is given a false account either of her age or of her appearance, he is entitled to have the marriage annulled.

The matrons arranging the marriage also negotiate the amount that the groom is to give the bride's parents, for in China the dowry is not paid by the father of the bride, but by the husband to his wife; to put it more bluntly, he purchases her. She becomes his property on two accounts. In some instances, however, a father may suggest that his future son-in-law come and live in his house, at the same time making him heir to part of his property, although he is not allowed to leave the remainder of his possessions to anyone outside his family or not bearing his name.

Fathers and mothers or close relations on the paternal side, and then those on the maternal side, enjoy absolute authority over the marriages of their children. There are only two cases in which sons are not subject to paternal authority: the first is if they marry a foreigner, for example a Jewess or a Muslem. Since foreigners live so differently from the Chinese, states the law, it is meet that a man entering into such an alliance should enjoy full freedom. Secondly, if a young man marries in a distant province during his travels, unaware that his family has entered into a commitment during his absence, his marriage will still be valid and he is not obliged to comply with the wishes of his father.

It is accepted practice among the wealthier classes that the terms of a marriage be established long before the future couple is old enough to wed; in some cases even before the intended are born.

When the two families have signed the contract and earnest money paid, thus formally entering into an engagement between the two, it is the daughter's family who names the day on which the marriage is to be celebrated. They consult the calendar with care to select the most propitious date, for there are good days and days of ill omen. During this period, the two families exchange presents. The groom sends his future bride jewels—rings, ear—rings, hair—pins. The two may write to each other but on no account may they see each other. The gifts and notes are transmitted by others.

During the three nights preceding the day on which the wedding is to be held, the whole of the inside of the bride's house is lit up, a sign of sorrow rather than of rejoicing: the parents, it is believed, should not be allowed to sleep when they are about to lose their daughter. In the same way, no musical instrument may sound in the groom's house, for the son's marriage is looked upon as presaging the death of the father and to a certain extent as signifying the son's succession to his parent.

On the day appointed for the marriage, the bridegroom, richly dressed, goes to his fiancée's house and kowtows to his father-in-law and mother-in-law, the uncles and the close relations of his bride. The bride, too, prostrates herself before all these relations as she makes ready to leave her paternal home.

When these preliminary formalities are complete, the fiancée is placed in a litter or enclosed palanquin. Everything she brings with her and her whole trousseau is also borne by various people of both sexes. Others

surround her with torches and lanterns, even in the middle of the day—a custom that been handed down from times when all marriages were celebrated at night. A troupe of musicians playing pipes, oboes and drums go before, followed by the family. The key used to lock her in the litter is held by a trusted servant; he must give it up to none other but the husband. After accompanying the procession for a time on horseback or in a palanquin, the groom goes on ahead so that he can await her at the gate where the procession is to arrive. He is handed the key; he hastens to open the litter and at first glance he sums up his fortune, assessing whether the account he has received of her has been faithful or exaggerated. On occasions, a disappointed bridegroom may shut the door again quickly and send the girl back home. He is allowed to reject her, provided that he agrees to forfeit the amount he has paid to obtain her.

If the bride receives his approval, she descends from the litter and enters the house with the bridegroom, each followed by their parents. They are ushered into a room where the newly united couple salutes the *Tiene* four times and then the husband's parents. The bridge and groom then repair to the place where a nuptial feast has been prepared for them alone. Before sitting down the bride genuflects four times before her husband and he in turn kneels twice before her; finally, they seat themselves at table, but before eating they pour a little wine as a libation and set aside a few items of food as an offering to the spirits. When they have eaten a little, the groom silently rises to his feet, invites his bride to drink and sits down again without having touched the wine; the bride then performs the same ceremony. Two cups of wine are then brought to them; they drink a little and mingle the remainder in a single cup, which they drain together.

During this time, the groom's father, in a nearby apartment, is giving a great feast to his family, and to his guests; the mother also entertains the women members of her

Right: scenes of conjugal or amorous intimacy.

24

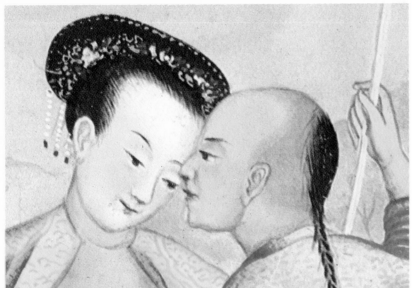

family and the wives of her husband's friends. This practice is common to all Chinese festivals.

In China, a man may have only one legitimate wife, but at the same time he is free to take several concubines. The ancient peoples introduced this custom for the sole purpose of increasing their population, and this is still the reason advanced by any Chinese man who wishes to preserve domestic harmony. The main argument he uses to win over his wife is that by taking concubines he can procure a greater number of women to serve her.

In other cases, the sole reason for a husband taking a concubine may be that he is anxious for a male child whom his legi-

timate wife is unable to bear him, and he will dismiss the other woman as soon as this end is achieved.

These concubines are usually taken from the cities of Yangchow and Soochow. There they are taught the art of pleasing, all the accomplishments that add to the natural grace of their sex: music, singing, dancing, the playing of instruments. Almost all these girls are born of slaves. They are bought and sold, a trade for which the two cities are famous.

The individual right to keep a concubine is tolerated by usage alone but is not authorised by law, which accords the privilege only to the emperor, princes of the blood

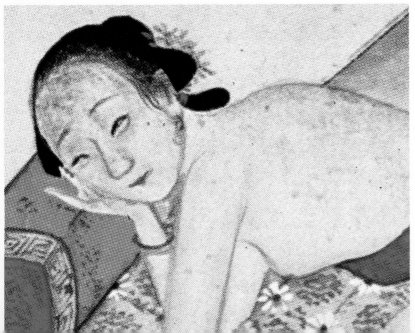

and mandarins; the emperor alone is formally entitled to have more than one concubine.

The Chinese wife is responsible for all the details of the home. She not only holds all the contracts, money and valuables, but she must watch over the internal management of her house, order all the purchases and preside over the household expenditure and the running of the household.

To justify their taking of concubines as well a wife, those of literary bent quote the authority of Confucius. When consulted on the point by his disciples, this philosopher replied in allegorical tone: "When the coat upon your back, is old, worn or no longer in fashion, do you not take another?" These same people, in support of their illustrious master's decision and to retain their freedom to use concubines, advance many other reasons, especially the following: "In China, many more girls are born than boys; what otherwise would become of this surplus?"

It should be noted that the use of concubines is not general. Chinese who prefer harmony to reign in their homes or who have no higher ambition to enjoy the pleasures of conjugal union, and those who still pride themselves upon their stringent moral standards, have only one legitimate wife.

The *Li-ki,* or books of rites, states that education begins from the moment of birth. This ancient book allows wet-nurses, but it enjoins mothers to take great care in their selection of one.

The child is weaned as soon as he can use his hands for eating, and he is taught to use his right hand. At the age of six, if he is a male, he is taught his numbers and the names of the principal parts of the universe. He is separated from his sisters at the age of seven and is no longer allowed to eat with them, or even to sit in their presence.

At eight, he is trained in the rules of courtesy; he is shown how to behave when he enters a house and when with old, or older people; at nine years old he is introduced

A house in the country. A mother teaching her son to walk; a baby in a rattan seat which closely resembles a model still in use in the West. Woman resting and dreaming on a divan (details from early engravings).

to the calendar system. At ten, he is sent to a public school. His masters will teach him to read, write and count. He studies music from the age of thirteen to fifteen, and all the words he chants express moral precepts.

Having reached the age of fifteen, a boy starts upon physical exercise, learning to draw the bow and ride a horse. At about the same time, if he is deemed worthy, he receives a hat which shows that he is admitted to the estate of manhood; from then on he is allowed to wear silk robes and furs, whereas previously he was entitled to no more than cotton garments.

From the elementary chapbook, he passes to the four books setting forth the doctrine of Confucius. The meaning of the work is explained to the child only when, in a sense, he knows the books by heart—in other words, when he is master of all the characters.

Chinese scholars attach great importance to the writing of characters, and this is why it is vital to the Chinese that young people receive early training in the art of calligraphy. Neatness, precision, elegance of characters: all these factors are weighed in the examination taken by pupils for promotion to higher classes.

In each town and even in the smallest villages, teachers are to be found who have set up school to initiate young children to the rudiments of human knowledge; in most cities, higher schools or colleges exist to teach all subjects, or at least those cultivated by the Chinese.

The education of young Chinese girls is aimed at inculcating a love of withdrawal, modesty and even silence. They are also encouraged to develop certain pleasing talents, if they are born rich. The general practice throughout the empire is that daughters at the age of seven are enclosed in the women's apartments, emerging only when they marry. No man may enter these apartments, and as the girls never leave them and are always supervised by their mother, their grandmother or their sisters, there is obviously no opportunity for loss of innocence If, however, it is found in a court of law that a girl has allowed herself to be "corrupted", her father and mother are punished as accomplices as well as the close relations, and

even the neighbours for not having denounced this crime. As for the girl, if it is ascertained that her consent had been given, she is publicly sold as a slave unless her seducer comes to claim her as his wife to evade the punishment he deserves. Such affairs always cause a great deal of scandal, the results being terrible; so they are indeed very rare.

Chinese ideas on what constitutes human beauty differ widely from our own. In China, a man is considered handsome if he has a wide forehead, a short nose, small, prominent, deeply slitted eyes, a wide, square face, large ears, a medium—sized mouth, a long beard and shining black hair.

In general, Chinese dress consists of a long tunic reaching to the ground; one flap—the left—of the tunic overlaps the other and is fastened on the right by four or five gold or silver buttons close to each other. The sleeves of this tunic are wide at the shoulder, narrowing as they reach the wrist. They are so long that they cover the hands, no more than the finger tips appearing at the horseshoe-shaped sleeve end. The Chinese wear a large silk belt about their waist, the ends hanging free to the knees. A kerchief, a bag and a little box containing a knife and the two chopsticks that are used in place of table implements are normally attached to this belt.

Peasants have a type of over-tunic that they wear in the rainy season which protects them from extremes in temperature. This tunic consists of a net through which are threaded various layers of unplaited reed or dry grasses. When the rain falls it does not penetrate this overmantle as the water runs down the outside of the grasses and keeps the wearer dry. A vast hat, made in the same way,˙ also protects his head and completes his rustic apparel.

In China the colour of mourning is white: a man's hat, his jacket, his overcoat, his stockings and his shoes will be made of common white material, roughly sewn. A hempen belt is tied around the jacket; in place of buttons and button holes there are frayed

Left: small table with bowl of fruit and vases; traditional decorative items from Chinese interiors. Facing: a) woman doing her hair in front of a mirror; b) female finery, curiously depicted on a fresco from Konsu (pre-Christian period).

29

strips of canvas knotted together. During the life of his father and mother, a son is not allowed to wear white; it is only at their burial that the children appear dressed in white, the clothes dirty and soiled with dust. To wear a cleaner garment would be of scandalous impropriety.

The Chinese have not always shaved their heads; indeed, they used to take the greatest care of their hair. When the Tartars became their masters, they obliged the Chinese to cut off most of their hair in accordance with their own custom.

The portion of hair that the Chinese retain on the top or the back of the head is made into a plait, normally very long, which they call the *pene-se*. The cap they wear is cone-shaped or like an inverted funnel.

A singular custom of the Chinese is that they allow their nails to grow to excessive lengths, some almost as long as the fingers themselves. This is not a custom of the nation at large but is limited to men, important personages and to scholars. They look upon these long nails as an adornment and also as an honourable distinction setting them apart from the common people, showing to all onlookers that they enjoy a position such as to have no need to engage in mechanical skills or to live from the labour of their hands.

Even the colour that a man of a given condition may wear is laid down by Chinese law. The emperor and princes of the blood alone are empowered to wear yellow. Certain mandarins may wear satin with a red background, but only on feast days; in everyday life, they are dressed in black, blue or violet. The colour usually worn by the ordinary people is black or blue and the fabric they use is never better than a simple cotton cloth.

Modesty is the prevailing note in the dress of women: their robes are closely buttoned to the neck, a white satin collar around their throat, and are so long that they cover even the tips of the feet. Over this dress, which is usually made of silk, is a species of overcoat whose sleeves would sweep the ground did they not take care to prevent it; but rarely are their hands to be glimpsed. A Chinese woman hides everything except her face.

The women are usually fairly small in height; the nose is short, the eyes small and she has a pretty mouth with crimson lips, black hair and largish ears. Their features are regular, their complexion is clear and their expression one of gaiety. Some of them allow their nails to grow. Most retain of their natural eyebrows only a thin, well-drawn line. Although stoutness is looked upon with approval in a man, they regard it as a great defect in their own sex and do all they can to keep their waist slim and their figure delicate.

Although they are condemned virtually never to leave their own apartments, many hours are devoted to their own toilet. Every day they rise, dress and spend hours before the mirror.

In former times the luxury of bathing was a common indulgence in China, especially among the great and in the palace of the emperors. In ancient times, Chinese women used aromatic and perfumed oils to anoint their bodies after the bath.

As soon as a Chinese female child is born, her feet are bound tightly with bandages and this type of torture is employed as long as the foot is likely to develop and grow. How much effort is demanded of a young child, how great must be her pain as she learns to stand to make her first few steps! No matter! She has been persuaded that a tiny foot is the most desirable attribute of a woman and the foundation of her beauty; no more than this budding coquetterie is needed to enable her to endure all to acquire such an inestimable prize. When she has achieved it, she will continue to suffer further pain to keep her feet so tiny. This long condition of discomfort and suffering appears to be tolerated by Chinese women by force of habit, and their health does not seem to be affected. They walk with difficulty, with faltering steps, but walk they do and it is rare indeed that they fail to seize an opportunity, despite their long robes, of furtively showing the tips of their pretty little satin slippers, almost always adorned with gold or silver embroidery. The bizarre custom established in a people so wise and so sage has led some to believe that it must be due to some secret political end, for instance that of

Terra cotta statuette of a serving girl (Tang period).

ensuring that women remain sedentary and obliging them to keep to their apartments. But is there any other people of Asia, a continent in which women are condemned to a life of the most stringent enclosure, who uses this expedient to keep their females in a state of submission?

Others attribute the origin of this Chinese passion for tiny feet to the empress Ta-ki. It would not be surprising if an empress, provided by nature with an extremely small foot had made this new form of coquetterie fashionable.

Women of the lower classes and those whose condition forces them to work in the fields know nothing of the use of these bonds and allow their feet to grow to their natural size, but they are disdained by their social superiors who pity them for the sad facility they have to walk so freely and easily!

Buildings in China, even the public monuments and imperial residences, are less striking for their magnificence than for their extensiveness. The emperor's palace at Pekin may be compared to a great city. The houses of princes, of the leading mandarins, of the wealthy, have as many as four or five forecourts and in each is a main building with three doors in the façade.

In ancient times, the Chinese were accustomed to build their houses facing south because they thought this to be more salubrious. This old usage became mandatory for palaces and was also adopted when constructing private houses; even in the cities, this exposure is sought, to the point of making roads irregular.

The courtyards take up more than half of the land used for the house; one leads on to another, with various apartments on either side. At the end of each of these forecourts is a pool of water with a pretty artificial rockery in the middle from which grow shrubs and several species of rock garden plants. These basins contain goldfish, which may be so tame that they come to the surface to be fed by human hand. In the centre of the court is a pedestal with a large porcelain vase in which are placed the most beautiful of flowers such as the peony. Other flower pots line the walls of the apartments and in the corners are little shrubs, vines or bamboos, forming areas of a soft green. Sometimes strange animals are also kept in these court-yards, as well as rare birds for the beauty of their plumage.

The main rooms and the outside rooms in each apartment are the reception rooms for visitors, a bedroom and a study or library.

The Chinese affect neither gilding nor mirrors nor tapestries in the decoration of their drawing rooms. The hangings favoured by the more wealthy are of white satin on which are painted birds, flowers, landscapes, mountains; often the artist will have inscribed in large blue characters verses, proverbs and maxims culled from the books of their philosophers. The poorer among them merely whitewash the walls of their rooms, while others line their walls with decorated paper.

A special kind of decoration are the pretty painted silk lanterns, often richly adorned, hung from the ceiling like chandeliers. In nooks and crannies of the apartments will be pedestal tables bearing bowls of lemons and other sweet smelling fruits.

The great droughts prevalent in China mean that the slightest breeze will raise and cause to hang in the air clouds of fine, impalpable dust, penetrating everywhere, even the most tightly sealed apartment. The brilliant polish imparted to Chinese tables and furniture by varnishing is ceaselessly dulled by this deposit of dust. The need to combat this nuisance caused by the climate obliges the Chinese to carry little feather dusters with which they dust and clear the inside of the apartments. These domestic implements, at first carried for practical reasons, have gradually become works of art and are as varied in their form as in the way in which they are made.

The Chinese bed, the central piece of funiture in the bedroom, is decorated according to the state and the means of the owner. In the houses of the great, the beds are often of extreme magnificence, being made of precious woods with lacquer or gilding. During the winter they are decked with satin-lined curtains, while in summer white taffeta hangings are used, with scattered images of birds and shrubs or gold-embroidered flowers. Less wealthy people are content with canvas hangings and their mattresses are merely stuffed with cotton.

In the northern provinces, the common people sleep on a bed of bricks, the width depending on the number of individuals in the family. They use a little stove nearby for heating, burning not wood but coal whose smoke is led out of the room by a pipe rising above the roof. On this stove they cook their food and heat their tea and even their wine, for the Chinese always prefer warm drinks, with the exception of a few iced refreshments taken during the burning heat of the summer.

The meals of people of superior rank may be sumptuous and great attention must be paid to manners. These are the rules of courtesy laid down by one of the Chinese classics: "When you receive someone or when you eat at his table, always abstain from eating with greed, from drinking long draughts, from making sounds with your mouth or your teeth, from gnawing on the bones and throwing them to the dogs; do not drink up the sauce remaining in the bowl or show that you desire such and such a dish or wine; do not clean your nails, nor serve yourself with a different sauce for the dish which has been set before you. Take only small mouthfuls, masticate your meat well and let not your mouth become over-full..."

The invitation ceremonial is complicated; it is assumed to be genuine only after it has been given up to three times in writing.

The tables are placed in two rows along the sides of the room, with a wide space in the middle, soon to be occupied by a troupe of players who will act a play designated by the chief guest after they have told him of their repertory.

A meal is begun not by eating but by drinking, and nothing but pure wine will be served. First of all the butler, kneeling on one knee, asks the guests to take up their cups, and each gathers it up with both hands, lifts it to his forehead, lowers it to below the level of the table and then raises it to his mouth. They drink all together, slowly, three or four times.

Picture, cord, vase, cup and casket: the traditional ornamentation of a window frame. Bottom: the stall of a lantern merchant, Peking.

32

During the time of drinking the various meats are placed on each table. Up to twenty four are offered to each guest, mainly in the form of blends. The Chinese do not use knives, but two little pointed sticks inlaid with ivory or silver which they use in place of forks. No guest begins to eat until he has been invited to do so by the butler, and the same rite occurs whenever the guest's cup is refilled with wine or a fresh course served.

The dessert, like the feast, consists of twenty to twenty-four dishes: sweatmeats, fruits, jams, ham, salt duck that has been cooked, or rather allowed to dry in the sun and finally small fish or shellfish.

These feasts begin towards the end of the day and end no sooner than midnight.

Each man then returns home in his litter, preceded by several servants bearing large paper lanterns on which are written the titles and sometimes the names of their master in large characters. Anyone daring to walk out at such an hour without this cortege would be arrested by the guard. The next day the host is invariably thanked by a written note.

The ceremonial meals such as we have described take place only in exceptional circumstances such as weddings, funerals, promotion to high office, the birth of a long-desired child or a sixtieth, seventieth or eightieth birthday.

The Chinese are born hospitable: they are polite, thoughtful, affectionate to their relations and their friends and affable to foreigners, taking a genuine pleasure in welcoming them whenever they come to their houses. Even the poorest of families seems rich when they wish to welcome a guest.

All manner of foods necessary for life are to be found in abundance in the immense soil of China. Rice is the staple food of the inhabitants of the southern provinces: together with rice, a large quantity of wheat is consumed in the North.

Apart from butcher's meat, the Chinese cook game, poultry, fish and water fowl. In the markets of Pekin are to be found pieces of venison piled high, sold throughout the winter; the cold and the nitrous air of this climate preserves the meats from deterioration. Even fish can be conserved there, the seas and rivers of China providing a multitude of species.

34

Butchers' shops are full of beef in the northern provinces, but this sort of meat is fairly rare in the South where few beef cattle are raised. Mutton is more common there and is acceptable on all tables. The Chinese prefer the meat of white sheep and regard it as vastly superior in texture and taste to that of black sheep. They scorn the flesh of sheep whose fleece contains two or more colours and suspect it of being unhealthy.

Of all the domestic animals of China the pig is the one which has multiplied the most, and its flesh is the most widely consumed. Among the ancient Chinese, fresh pork was no longer eaten as soon as the first heat of summer set in but during this interval its salted and smoked flesh used to be served on all tables. Even today, Chinese doctors prescribe ham for stomachs tired and weakened by the excessive heat.

An emperor, Kan-hi, an enlightened gour-

Left : meal outdoors. Bottom : a lady of the aristocracy drinking her tea which has been prepared and served by two maids. Below : traditional greetings.

met, liked to eat stag tongues and tails. To these luxury foods should be added the nerves of stags and birds nests. These nests are built by a particular species of swallow; they are boiled to reduce them to white threads like vermicelli; then anything black or unclean is removed and they are placed in an ordinary meat or chicken broth. Prepared in this way and seasoned in proper proportions by selected spices and aromatic herbs, they are ready to be served. Such food, it is said, provides an abundance of prolific juices and perhaps it is to this reputedly aphrodisiac property that birds nests owe their fame and this is why they are sought so eagerly.

Other dishes also appear on the tables of the wealthy, and these may be very strange: a mandarin may, for example, eat and prize shark's fins, the flesh of the wild mare, bear paws, the feet of wild animals.

The Chinese consume an enormous quantity of vegetables, eating far more of these than of meat. This taste for grasses, roots and seeds is to an extent a national habit, shared by all conditions of men.

The general custom is to eat meat only on days of public rejoicing and at special family feasts. During the remainder of the year, it is eaten only twice a month and always at a single meal; only rarely and under exceptional circumstances are children and young people allowed to eat meat.

The blending of meats with various species of vegetable is one of the special features of Chinese cuisine. The Chinese are convinced that certain dishes are improved and more healthy when they are cooked with a certain other meat or herb or seed or root. For example, they eat the flesh of the deer or the hare together with pork, mutton with cabbage, etc. Meats are always cut into tiny slices or threads before cooking; the chef's art and skill lie in knowing which can be combined and the proper proportion of the mixture.

Chinese gastronomes have advanced their study of the art of cooking to such a point that they maintain that the true savour of foods will be tasted only if they are cooked on a certain type of fire.

They prefer, for example, a mulberry wood fire for boiled chicken which they claim makes it more tender; acacia wood is used to cook pork to give it more taste and render it more digestible; pine is employed to heat water for tea, and so on.

The Chinese eat twice a day, the first meal being at ten in the morning, the second at six in the evening.

The emperor himself presides over the feasts which hail the arrival of spring. One feast day celebrated by the Chinese with great rejoicing is the New Year. The holiday begins on the eve of New Year, the last day of the twelfth month. All business, both of the government and of the nation, is suspended. The lower ranks of the mandarins go to salute their superiors; the children perform the same duty to their fathers, the servants to their masters. All the families gather together in the evening to present compliments and congratulations to each other, terminating with a great meal: it is called "bidding farewell to the year". The ensuing two or three days are filled with games and festivals and entertainment. Everyone wears his richest apparel; visits are paid to neighbours, friends and protectors. Congratulations and gifts are exchanged and protestations of friendship are loaded on each other.

But the most brilliant of the Chinese festivals, the day celebrated with greatest joy, pomp and expenditure, is the festival of the lanterns. This is held on the fifteenth day of the first month, but it begins on the evening of the thirteenth day and ends far in the night of the sixteenth. It is a general holiday and during these three or four nights the whole of China seems to be ablaze. The towns, villages, sea shores, edges of the roads and rivers are bedecked with countless lanterns of all sizes and shapes. In towns, roads, public places, the fronts and court-yards of the palaces are decorated with these lights; they are to be seen at every door and

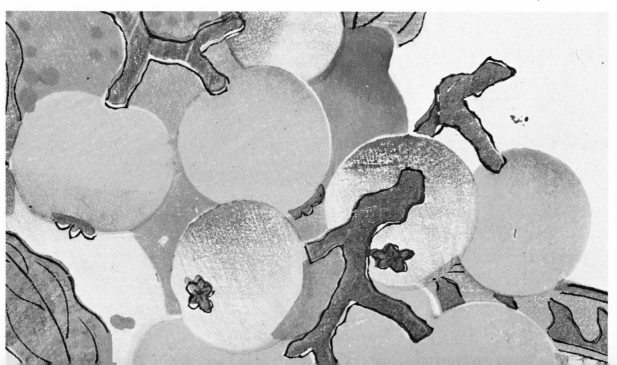

at the windows of even the poorest houses. All the sea ports are illuminated by the lanterns hung from the masts and from the rigging of the Chinese junks and erected on the sand bars. In this festival, probably more than two hundred million lanterns are lit: the rich vie in the magnificence of this type of illumination and try to outdo each other in the beauty of the lanterns hung before their houses; those commissioned by the great mandarins, the viceroys and the emperor himself are so finely worked that each one costs a substantial sum.

All the marvels of the pyrotechnic art are combined with those of illumination to rejoice the heart during these nocturnal festival. No Chinese man of means fails to prepare a few fireworks; all let off at least a few rockets and squibs, clouds of stars and raining sparks light up the air and fire the sky.

The month of November also brings with it another festival, again a time of diversion and entertainment for the Chinese. This feast, held after all the harvests have been brought in, is intended to celebrate the constant fertility of the soil and the end of the year's labours by thanks and public rejoicing. It lasts more than fifteen days and plays are enacted to add to the joy of the festivals.

These autumn rejoicings are the favourite of the Chinese women, for they are allowed to go out and walk in the streets, a pleasure in which they delight despite the discomfort of their tight shoes.

Puppet-players abound in China; as in all countries where discipline is strict, there are many amusements for the children.

Hunting, a sport indulged in by the nobility of Europe, is a common pleasure in China.

Fishing is a trade and industry rather than an amusement. The Chinese fish in different ways: the use nets to take up large quantities of fish, a rod for individual fish.

Another sort of fishing, known only in their country although it is so simple in

Left: this allegorical composition, a plate from the famous Kempfer Series, in the British Museum, is a fine example of the delicate art of the Chinese print. Facing, top: imperial festivities; bottom: Emperor Yeou, "who lost the Empire because he tried to induce laughter in a woman whom nothing could make to laugh".

principle, is to nail a wide board painted bright white from one end of a long boat to the other; this board slopes almost to the surface of the water. It is used only at night when the boat is turned so that the light of the moon is reflected from the white board. The fish cannot distinguish between the painted board and the water and leap up to fall in the hull.

The Chinese have played chess from time immemorial. The chess board they use consists of sixty four squares but is not divided into black and white. They do not place the pieces in the squares but in the corner of the squares, in other words at the points of intersection. The chess board is divided into two halves, each containing thirty two squares for each of the two players, and these two halves are separated by a space known as the *river*. This space is the same width as a row of squares and runs crosswise across the board.

Chinese kites are finer than in any other country in the ingeniousness of their composition: they may take the most varied and pleasant of forms, with rich, bright colours. Sometimes they may be fashioned in the image of an immortal majestically borne aloft upon a cloud; sometimes they represent birds of prey, winged dragons, bright coloured butterflies, animals, monsters.

The Chinese also have skates during the winter and are skilful in skimming over the surface of the ice.

One visit in China is an affair of great weight, entailing preliminaries unknown elsewhere or which have now been done away with: it is the visit paid to the governor of the town in which one dwells, and it is always accompanied by the offering of fairly substantial presents. It is customary to present a long painted box decorated with gold painted flowers, the inside divided into eight or twelve small compartments, each filled with a different form of dry comfit. When one approaches the great mandarin, one is expected to bow deeply, kneeling and bending one's head to the ground until one is invited to rise. Sometimes the governor is offered a cup filled with wine saying the words, as a greeting: "here is the wine which brings happiness, the wine which brings long life". Such are the words spoken as one

proffers the gift that one has brought.

The occasions on which, according to Chinese etiquette, mutual visits are paid and presents exchanged, depending on the taste or needs of the person visited, are the beginning of each year, certain feasts, the marriage of a friend, the birth of a son, promotion to some office, the death of a member of a family or the undertaking of a long journey.

The exchange of correspondence, even among ordinary individuals, is governed by its own formalities, becoming more complicated when writing to a person of stature. Then white paper must be used with ten to twelve folds; the letter is begun on the second and the writer's name is appended only on the last page.

The characters used may differ according to the circumstances: the smaller it is, the more respectful is it considered. The terms used, the distances left between lines, are also dictated by the rank of the person to whom they are addressed. But the style always differs from that of ordinary conversation. A sort of bag serves as an envelope for the missive; this is bordered by a pretty edging and can be found ready made. In China, it is the normal practice for this "envelope" to be two-fold: on the inner is written the words: "the letter is within". The packet is inserted into a second, thicker envelope which in itself is partly wrapped around with a strip of red paper on which bearing the name and title of the person to whom the letter is addressed. At the side, in smaller characters is written the province, the town and the place of residence and finally the date of the letter. The ends of the envelope are then brought together and a seal affixed with these words: "protected and sealed".

The Chinese fashion of greeting, even between individuals of a fairly low estate, is characteristic: a bow, a nod or a tilt of the hat is not sufficient. An ordinary greeting consists of joining one's hands, moving them in an affectionate manner and inclining one's head a little, saying "tsin-tsin", words that

11th-century painting entitled "The Return from the Feast" (Boston, Museum of Fine Arts); statuette of a person whistling (Yuan period); detail from the "thousand deer" decorative motif on a large Ming vase (Musée Guimet, Paris).

mean anything one wishes, to each other. On encountering a person of a senior rank, one must join one's hands, raise them above one's forehead, lower them to the ground and bow from the waist.

If two acquaintances meet after a fairly lengthy absence, they fall to their knees in front of each other, then bow to the ground, stand up and begin the same ceremony over again, repeating it up to two or three times.

The death of a Chinese is commonly a day of honour for him: never does he receive so much attention, so much homage, so many marks of esteem as when he is no more.

Rarely is the dead man washed; a few moments after life has left his body, he is dressed in his richest garments and the symbol of his dignity. He is then placed in the coffin which has just been purchased for him or which he himself has had made in advance, a strange form of forethought but one common to this people.

One of the main subjects of preoccupation

to a Chinese is to prepare his coffin so that this burden does not devolve upon his heirs. Even those who have hardly any money will devote most of what little they have to this purchase. Sometimes the coffin remains in the house for twenty years before use, and in the eyes of the master it will be the most valuable of the furnishings. If he has not already made arrangements and if no other means of buying a coffin exists, the son— through filial respect—may sell himself or enlist so that he may procure a coffin worthy of his father. They may be found ready made on the premises of tradesmen and these lugubrious objects, which in all other countries are hidden from view, often form the main objects of display in certain shops. It is far from rare that private persons of substantial means lay out a small fortune to procure a coffin in precious wood with carvings, richly painted and gilded.

Chinese may carry filial attachment so far as to keep the corpse of their father in the home for three or four years. No magistrate is entitled to force the family to bury a member. The air in the house is not affected since the thick wood of which the coffins are made so well lined with pitch and bitumen that the foetid air cannot escape. Apart from the general obligations of mourning, anyone keeping the body of his father will have special duties; he will have no other chair to sit on during the day than a stool covered in white serge and no other bed than a simple rush mat placed beside the coffin.

If the burial is to take place immediately after the death, it is normal practice for the corpse to be exposed for seven days, although this may be reduced to three for any pressing reason. During this time, all the family and friends, who are personally invited, come to pay their respects to the deceased. The closest relations even stay in the house. The coffin is placed in the ceremonial room which has been hung with white; a few pieces of black or violet silk are mingled with this colour as well as certain other ornaments used for mourning. Before the coffin is placed a table on which rests the picture of the dead man or a card bearing his name, always accompanied by flowers and perfumes.

The custom is to salute the coffin as if the person it encloses were still alive. Deep

bows are made before the table and each visitor strikes the floor several times with his forehead. Then perfumes and candles brought with each visitor are placed upon the table. The special friends or those reputed to be so moan and groan in a more or less sincere fashion during these ceremonies.

The greetings that they have come to pay to the corpse are returned by the eldest son together with his brothers who emerge from behind a curtain at the side of the coffin. They do not walk but crawl on the ground, dragging themselves to the sides of those whom they wish to greet. Another curtain also conceals the women who every now and then give out the most dismal of wailing.

Those coming to pay their last respects to the dead man are then conducted to another apartment where they are offered tea, dried fruits and other similar refreshments. A distant relation or a friend of the family is then made responsible for doing the honours, receiving and accompanying the visitors to the door.

The family and friends are informed of the date appointed for the funeral.

The cortege is led by a group of men walking in single file bearing various paper board statues: some may represent slaves, others tigers, lions, horses, etc. Other groups follow, walking in two files, carrying long painted boards on which are inscribed the titles of the dead man. Others bear aloft standards or burners giving off the odour of perfumes. Musicians play many instruments, the airs they choose being mournful. Music forms a part in all the funeral ceremonies of ancient peoples. The musicians immediately precede the coffin, which is covered with a dome-shaped dais, made of a richly edged violet silk stuff; its four corners are surmounted by the same number of white silk crests. The coffin is laid on a device borne by sixty four men. The eldest son, wearing a hempen sack, supporting himself on a stick, his body bent, closely follows the coffin and is himself followed by his brothers and nephews, although none wear a sack like him.

Chinese burial grounds are outside the towns, usually on the heights. As with many other peoples, it is customary to plant pines and cypresses at that place. The design of the tomb differs from province to province and according to the state and the fortune of those whose mortal remains have been placed therein. The poor merely place the coffin under a straw roof; others make a small brick hut in the shape of a tomb. The more well-to-do citizens build their sepulchres with taste, painting them white or blue, surrounding them with fencing in the same kind of metal used to shoe horses. The family's name is inscribed on the main stone.

Facing : percussion device used during funeral ceremonies (Chou period). Below : branch with flowers (Kempfer Series). Following pages : harnessed chariot (bronze, about 100 AD).

籬邊高致
冷靜伴書
畫屏亮

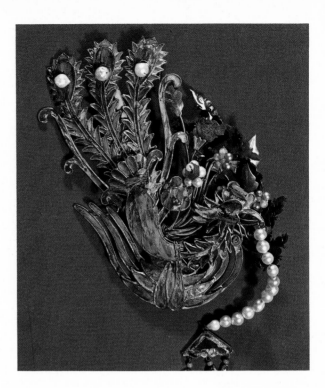

4

Astronomy is a very ancient science in China and probably dates back to the foundation of the empire. The first mention we have of it can be found in the *Yao-tien* chapter of the *Chu-kin,* where the emperor Yao (whose reign began in the year 2357 B.C.) teaches his astronomers Hi and Ho how to recognize and determine the four seasons.

A little more recently, though in the XIII century, Co-cheu-kin was one of the ablest astronomers China has ever produced. Kublai Khan, founder of the Mongol dynasty, had him brought to his court and appointed him chief mathematician. In 1280 he was able to identify the Winter solstice by using a huge gnomon and measuring the length of the shadow up to the centre of the projection or image of the sun which was thrown onto the surface.

Co-cheu-kin watched the movements of the polar star over a long period of time and was thus able to calculate that its distance from the pole was a little over three Chinese

Left: tablets depicting ancestors. Above: buckle which once belonged to an empress.

degrees; he was, in fact, the first mathematician in that country to use spherical trigonometry and the resolution of triangles in astronomy.

The path of the sun among the stars was known from the most ancient times and care was always taken to distinguish the ecliptic from the equator. The first was called *hoan-tao* or *yellow way,* while the second became known as *che-tao* or *equinoctial line* because it was known that this great celestial sphere is at an equal distance between the two poles and when the sun crosses the equator the day and night are everywhere of equal length.

The geometrical properties of the triangle and the rectangle, the discovery of which brought such honour to Pythagoras, were known in China long before this philosopher came to teach the Greeks about them. This knowledge of geometry is such an ancient one in China that even Emperor Khan-hi said it was impossible to establish in which period it originated.

It is fairly generally agreed that the Chinese invented the compass, and any others who may make claims for the glory of this discovery cannot have any good grounds for such an assertion. There is a general consensus among Chinese scholars on the attribution of the first use of the magnetic needle to the famous Prince Cheu-kon, brother of the Cheu emperors, who died twelve centuries ago.

However, several historians consider that the compass was invented even earlier than this, probably in the year 2600 B.C., by Emperor Hoan-ti who was well known for his scientific experiments.

It seems certain that the Arabs were familiar with the use of the compass long before the Europeans, and this knowledge was probably gained from the Chinese with whom they had traded for several centuries before the first ships from the West finally succeeded in rounding the Cape of Good Hope.

The study of medicine dates back to the early days of the Chinese empire. Though their doctors were never very expert in anatomy nor in the prescribing of cures, they still succeeded in making considerable progress which astounded western doctors.

It was their respect for the dead, based on filial piety, which discouraged them from the study of anatomy and filled them with disgust at the thought of having to dissect bodies. Of course this point of view could also be found in several other countries.

In spite of this repugnance for dissection, there is a mention in history books of the governor of a province who had the abdomen opened of fourty villanous men who had themselves opened the bellies of pregnant women and some children too, then he employed several painters to make accurate drawings of their intestines in the presence of learned physicians who were authorized to instruct the torturers on where to make their cuts and so to profit from the just torture of these men for the sake of progress in medical science.

In any case, their success and the precision with which they operated makes it clear that Chinese physicians must indeed have had some familiarity with human anatomy. It is true that they never did systematic dissections, nor did they ever open up dead bodies; but if they did neglect the study of dead creatures, they certainly made up for it by long, careful and deep examination of living nature which, even after thirty centuries, still yields up its secrets.

If the Chinese had really had no knowledge of the structure of the human body, how could they have discovered the circulatory system so many centuries before the rest of the world?

Chinese medicine is almost entirely empirical and therefore based on real experience. They have the greatest confidence in their herbal remedies which do no doubt have their effectiveness, but their skill consists in knowing how to administer them as effectively as possible and most of these remedies consist of decoctions and strong infusions. Still now, the doctors prescribe restoratives made of a mixture of herbs and fruits which they consider are necessary to eradicate a disease. Chemical preparations are virtually unknown to them.

The technique of measuring the pulse rate, practised in China for so many

Left : specimens of Chinese characters. Right : Chinese compasses from various periods (Peking, Museum of the People).

centuries and still considered an important means of diagnosis, attracted the attention of doctors first in Europe and then in the New World. Many of them set to deepening their knowledge of this science and agreed that it would indeed be a useful way to diagnose an illness or foretell the coming of a crisis. Finally, they are responsible for the great success of acupuncture all over the world.

The marvellous secret of the silk worm was transmitted to Italy by the Greeks, who received it from the peoples of the East, especially the Persians. According to the testimony of some of the best-known Oriental writers, the Persians drew their own knowledge of the precious insect from the Chinese themselves. China, then, appears to have been the original home of the silk worm. The care devoted to its raising and breeding, the growing of the mulberry tree on which it feeds and the fabrication of silks have grown

at a prodigious rate in this empire over the centuries, and the production of silks appears today to be inexhaustible.

The finest and the most highly regarded silk in the whole of the empire comes from the province of Chekiang.

Rich gold-embroidered materials appear to have been known in China in very ancient times, since they are mentioned in a Chi-kin ode dating from 781 B.C. Some scholars even maintain that they were invented much earlier, attributing their origin to the famous Choukon, who lived at the beginning of the 11th century B.C.

Fabric dying has been an art in China

Above : two plates from the Book of the Silk Industry *(early 19th century); the collection of the mulberries and the sorting of cocoons. Following pages : the training of the worms (same collection). Facing : woman cutting a piece of silk (early engraving).*

大凡至八蠶小繭
主繭埔繭板筑拈
茶收梌龍何用冬
共作綵絲與児與
素束枚帛非不熊
衷束枚帛非不熊
俗多稙祝鱼

from very ancient times. During the first three dynasties this was not a craftsman's work, but every family dyed its own cloths and silks. It was a task that devolved upon the women, as was the work of breeding silk worms, weaving the fabrics and making up the clothes.

Although porcelain has become one of the most illustrious branches of Chinese industry and trade, far less is known about its history than about many other of the people's arts. The inventor of porcelain is unknown; it may have been due to chance or it may have evolved from conscious strivings. It is not even possible to determine exactly how far it dates back. All that is known is that, according to the annals of Feou-lin, a very small town, one of whose districts is Kin-te-chin, the workers in this district have supplied china to the emperors since the year 442 A.D., one or two mandarins being appointed by the court to supervise its

49

Left: scene of spinning and weaving depicted on the top of a bronze casket (Han period; People's Republic of China). Bottom: decorative motifs on a 7th-century fabric (Sinkiang).
This page: musical scenes from a moving painting in the Museum of the Palaces, Peking; bottom: terra cotta depicting a harpist; an emperor listening to one of his female musicians (late 6th century); a flutist (embroidery on silk).

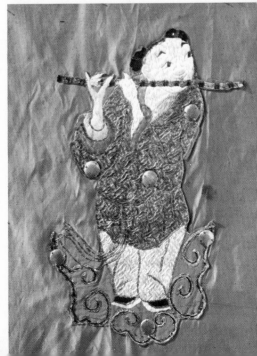

production. It is thought, however, that it was made well before this time and an expert has asserted that china was known at least since the Han dynasty, which dates from the year 202 B.C. Had it been developed to the fine craft we know today? To judge by the antique pieces that have been conserved in museums, the porcelain was not so transparent but the glazing was more beautiful and the colours livelier and brighter.

After a piece of china is made, it is passed to the "hoa-pei" or porcelain painters, who enjoy little more status than labourers. They do not work to rules, nor have they been taught the principles of drawing. Their whole science is no more than routine sparked by a curious imagination. Many are able tastefully to depict flowers, animals and landscapes both on porcelain and on paper fans and muslin for lanterns. In these workshops, the decoration is shared among many workers; one may be responsible solely for tracing the first coloured circle near the rim of a vase, while another draws the flowers, later coloured by a third; one man may specialise in water and mountains, another in birds and other animals.

The icing over of water in winter was the inspiration for Chinese artists to produce what we know as "crackle-ware". They used an oil paint which has the curious property of making it seem that the ware to which it is applied is criss-crossed with an infinity of cracks of hairlines. From a distance, such a vase looks as if it had been shattered but with all the pieces in place.

In former times Chinese craftsmen could produce an even more singular porcelain: on the walls of a vase they would paint fish, insects or other animals that could be seen only when the vase was filled with liquid. This secret is now almost lost, although some of the processes used are still known.

The Chinese classify their porcelain in several categories, depending on the fineness and beauty. All first class porcelain is reserved for the emperor. If one of these works comes into the hands of a commoner, it is because it is spoiled by stains or imperfections and is not considered fit to be offered to the sovereign.

China of average or ordinary quality is used in abundance by all classes of society.

It decorates apartments, offices, dressing tables, sideboards and even the kitchens. All persons of a certain wealth and even many of the ordinary people drink and eat from porcelain. It is the substance of which a host of little items of furnishing are made: urns, waste paper baskets, flower vases, small basins for goldfish. Architects even use it to cover the elegant roofing of certain buildings, sometimes instead of marble, incrusting the facades with china. In the country, there exist very tall towers entirely faced with china, the Nankin tower being reputedly the most beautiful.

Foreigners arriving in China are usually struck by the brilliance and beauty of the artifical flowers that are made there, which at first sight they all take to be real. This minor craft in which the Chinese seem to excel over all rivals has become a highly productive branch of industry occupying a host of people of both sexes and forming the basis of a profitable trade. An enormous number of such flowers is used and they are one of the most common of female adornments, usually being worn in the hair. The Chinese fashion artificial flowers from many materials, but for the more beautiful they choose a substance produced in their own territory and known only to themselves. Neither silk, nor cotton, nor any kind of fabric or paper enters into the composition of these inimitable flowers. The transparent, slender substance forming the corolla and the leaves is the pith of a certain bush or type of reed that grows in the province of Szechwan, which the Chinese call *ton-tsao*.

Chinese historians say that the year 105 A.D. marked the discovery of paper and its production for the first time. Before then, the Chinese used to write on fabric and silks, giving rise to the custom, which still exists, of writing maxims and moral sayings on large panels of silk and hanging them inside the houses, or praises of the dead to be suspended beside the coffin and borne aloft in funeral ceremonies. Even further

Chinese vases from various periods, interesting on account of their decorative motifs, and sample of crackled porcelain.

55

back, a cutting tool was used to write on tree bark, bamboo boards or even metal plates. Several of these tablets, threaded together, formed a book.

Chinese writers are not in agreement on the material used to form these boards at the time when they were first introduced; some believe that they were made solely of bamboo, while others assert that they could be of bamboo or any other type of wood. These boards were known by many names depending on the shapes and their final purpose. They were called "*tse*" when they were used for fairly substantial works; when assembled by means of a strap they formed a book and on the first of the boards were written the first few words of the work or the subject or merely the title.

These were the materials used before paper was invented. But the weight and volume of these tablets and the cost of the taffeta used to trace the characters made such writings either awkward to handle or costly. Finally, under the reign of Han-ho-ti, in about 105 B.C., a Chinese mandarin called Tsai-lung evolved a new substance that he thought might be easier to write upon. He took the barks of various trees, hemp trimmings, worn linen and old nets, boiled them separately to turn them into a sort of broth and combined them to form paper, which was first called after the name of its inventor. Little by little Chinese industry improved on this wonderful discovery, discovering the secret of bleaching, polishing and glazing, the different types of paper.

For many years the fineness, softness and strength of Chinese paper led Europeans to believe that it was made with silk. In fact, Chinese use substances derived from the bamboo, from cotton trees, from the bark of the tree known as "*choo-kou*" and mulberry bark, hemp, rice flakes, parchment from silkworm cocoons and many other substances, most of them unknown in Europe.

No type of paper is more widely used in China than bamboo paper. When selecting the bamboo shoots for paper, according to

Below : ornamented ceramic vase. Right : the Honan grotto decorated with statues of the defenders of Buddha.

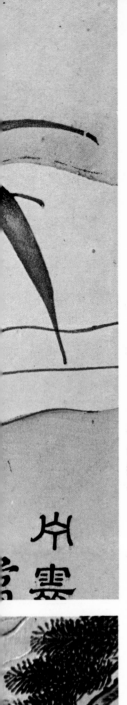

the Chinese maxim, one must "separate the ancestors from their descendants"—in other words, one must not mix old bamboo with new. New shoots that have grown during the past year are cut, selecting those whose bark has already formed.

Chinese ink is not liquid but is made up into tablets or sticks. The use of ink to trace characters was known in China more than ten centuries before the birth of Christ, but it was not the same ink as we know today. History tells us that, in about 620 A.D., the king of Korea, among the gifts he sent each year as a tribute to the emperor of China, offered him several pieces of ink made from a lamp black collected from some old pines that had been burned down, mixed with stag horn glue to make it into a solid paste. This ink was so bright that it could be taken for paint. For many years the Chinese tried to discover the process used by the Koreans and many tests were conducted, finally leading to success. Although they produced a good quality ink, only in about 900 A.D. did they achieve that degree of perfection that has ever since been characteristic of China ink.

Printing has existed in China for many centuries. According to one scholar, credit for this outstanding invention should go to the later Han dynasty, which was founded in the year 221 A.D. and lasted only forty three years. In China, however, the printing process is very different from our own. We have few letters in our alphabet and we need to found only an equivalent number of movable characters: suitably arranged and combined, these are sufficient to print very large volumes. Once a page has been printed, the type can be broken up and the same characters used to print the next page. This is not possible in China, where there are vast numbers of characters and it would be quite out of the question to found sets of sixty to eighty thousand characters. How

could they be arranged in the type case, even were this possible, and where would one find the space for all the type cases that would be needed?

This is how the Chinese print their books: they call in an excellent scribe who transcribes the book onto thin, transparent sheets of paper. The engraver glues each sheet onto a board made of timber from the apple or pear tree, or any other hard wood. With an engraver's tool, he traces the outlines of the strokes and cuts the characters in relief, cutting away all the wood in between. Each page of a book requires its own board.

The beauty of the type will thus depend on the skilled hand of the copyist, and whether a book is well or badly printed will depend on whether a good or a mediocre writer has been employed. The skill and precision of the engraver are so great that he will faithfully reproduce the original, and it is often difficult to distinguish the printed from the handwritten work. Obviously this method forestalls any typographical errors.

One of the first crafts evolved in China was that of metal casting. History tells us that Emperor Hoan-ti in the year 2622 B.C. had twelve bells cast whose sounds were graduated. They were called the twelve "lu" and they were used to calibrate the five musical keys. In one of his voyages, the emperor discovered a mine rich with copper and stayed in the canton long enough to establish a foundry where he had these large instruments made, furnishing the models himself. The bells are still the basis of the Chinese musical system and since ancient times they have provided the signals used by armies.

The Chinese undoubtedly knew about gunpowder before Europe, but it is difficult to determine the precise date of this invention. In 1621, the Portuguese from the city of Macao presented Emperor Hi-Tson with three large cannons, accompanied by their gun crews. They were taken to Pekin where they were tried out in the presence of the whole court and a vast crowd of spectators. An accident produced both awe and admiration: a Portuguese and three Chinese did not move away quickly enough and were killed by the recoil. The terrible effect of these machines led to the decision that they

Left : bamboo — a plant which was so valuable for writing and prints (plant from the famous collection The Ten-Bamboo Studio, *in the British Museum). Bottom: man of letters reading.*

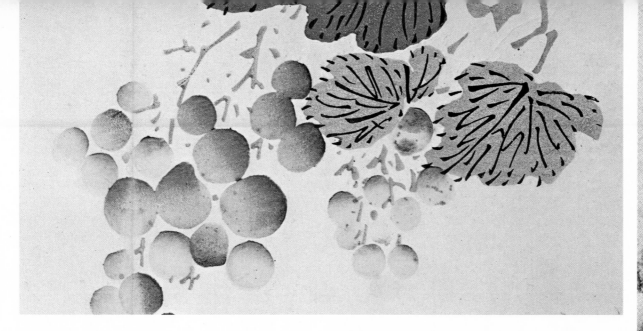

should be used against the Tartars, with whom China was at war at the time, and they were taken to the frontier.

From these and similar facts it appears that, when the Europeans were first allowed to enter their ports, the Chinese had only a limited concept of artillery and it did not form part of their armies. But other facts prove that they had previously known about fire arms and had used such devices and arms several centuries before gunpowder was discovered in Europe.

Wine made from grapes was known in China for centuries before the Christian era. Emperor Kan-hi observed, in his *Familiar Instructions,* that at first it served only for sacrifices and that for many years thereafter its use was extended only to revive the strength of the elderly, to receive guests with honour and to spread sweet gaiety in certain ceremonial feasts. In meetings between princes or during the visits of noblemen to the courts of emperors, wine was served but it was a rigid rule of etiquette that no more than three glasses should be drunk. According to other old books, it appears that the fashion in which wine was made at the time was generally the same as for the Greeks and Romans. One of the properties of this wine was that it could be kept for many years in urns buried underground.

Either for political motives, to prevent the disorders that might have ensued had the populace taken to wine-drinking, or from sheer necessity in order to provide sufficient food for a growing population, the growing of vines was often prohibited in China and their uprooting to make way for other edible crops ordered by public decree. These edicts, published so often and so sweeping in nature, had the effect in the long run of wiping out all memory of the vine and its fruit. The Chinese were then forced to indulge in spirits known to their ancestors from the very earliest of times. These were produced by fermentation of many different sorts of grain and led to the type of Chinese wine still popular today,

This "pseudo-wine" is really a beer produced by fermenting a mixture of water and grain.

True Chinese wines vary widely, depending on the ingredients added during the time of preparation—selected herbs, flavourings, honey, sugar, fruit (fresh or sun-dried).

Corn spirit has not been made for such a long time in China, since reliable scholars date its invention only to the end of the thirteenth century. Nonetheless, brandy made from grapes was celebrated in seventh century verse and works of medicine dating from the eleventh century prescribed it as an excellent remedy for sores, bruises and certain internal diseases.

The types of grain at first used for the production of this "eau-de-vie" were wheat, rice and millet. It was, however, a consistent aim of Chinese policy that the use and consumption of these grains, so necessary for

Above and right: bunch of grapes and lychees (plates from the Ten-Bamboo Studio). *Facing: pastoral figure, detail from an early engraving.*

the subsistence of the people, be restricted by law. Today most of the spirits manufactured in the northern provinces are based on sorghum, and in the southern provinces on a wild rice known as *kian-mi,* together with sugar cane.

Chinese spirits are bitter but they are very much to the taste of the Chinese people who always drink them hot, often throwing moderation to the winds. Some individuals, indeed, drink spirits only if they have been twice distilled.

The Chinese still use a special wine it is beyond the imagination of Europeans to conceive: *lamb wine.* It is very strong but the odour it gives off is unpleasant and repellent. The same may be said of a sort of brandy based on the flesh of mutton.

5

The Chinese nation is too old and too religiously attached to its ancient usages for its architecture not to be influenced by that of its earliest times, and the observant eye will note upon it the imprint of great antiquity. As in the ancient monuments of Egypt, they have conserved a taste for the pyramid and frequently build columns that are used solely as supporting pillars. Although the art has not achieved the degree of perfection reached by the Greeks and the Romans, it is difficult not to notice the great beauty of detail, the occasional boldness and in all cases an astonishing grandeur in the order and proportions of Chinese buildings. The imperial residences are true palaces; the immensity, symmetry, elevation and magnificence of the buildings of which they are composed announce the greatness of the master who dwells within. The Paris Louvre would easily fit into a single one of the many courts in the Pekin palace.

In Peking. Left : the Forbidden City; above : decorative motifs of the Temple of Heaven.

Chinese architecture is quite unconnected with that of the West. Under different skies, it has had to follow different laws, accommodating to the climate and the physical properties of the soil. The practice of architecture is by no means a matter of slavish routine; it too has its principles, its rules, its proportions.

Almost every house and every building is made of wood and brick. It is not that China contains no marble or stone, since most provinces are rich with such materials and many towns are paved with multi-coloured marbles. Nor is it the difficulty of conveyance. The imperial gardens are strewn with giant rocks and the palaces are constructed on immense marble block and alabaster foundations; all the steps of the staircases, however long and however wide, are made of single blocks. Nor is it the difficulty of cutting stone, since stone is employed in many public structures and many tombs are stone throughout, even the leaves of the doors. The need to take precautions against earth tremors has no doubt had an important influence on the Chinese style of building, but the main reason preventing the use of marble and stone is that the heat and humidity of the southern provinces and the extreme cold of the north would make such houses unhealthy and almost uninhabitable. Even in Pekin, where

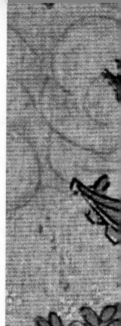

the rainy season lasts only a short while, it is found necessary to lay felt strips on the small marble staircases in the palace; the humidity in the air makes everything damp and run with water. During the winter, the cold is so acute that the ice does not melt during more than three months and no window can be opened on the northern side.

The same reasons, based on the climate, also make it impossible to build storeys; a second or a third floor could be inhabited neither during the heat of the summer nor during the extreme cold of winter.

Nonetheless, multi-storeyed buildings were fashionable in China for many centuries when the imperial court resided in the southern provinces. Almost all the little palaces erected by the emperors in their gardens were of this kind.

The whole of China provides a soil suitable for the brick buildings so common there. The bricks are of roughly the same size as in other countries, and are placed to dry in the sun or fired in a kiln. Bricks to be used for public buildings are often decorated on the outside with drawings and carefully worked relief figures.

It is to the Chinese that we owe the invention of double roofs, one of the most noble and richest ornaments of their great architecture. These roofs do not rest on the walls but on columns forming a picturesque and effective "crown". Neither the Greeks nor the Romans were ever to use the roof to the full for it was a structural element that evaded their skills. Italian architects, despairing of

making them beautiful, seem to have taken the easy way out by concealing them. The Chinese had greater address: they have succeeded in covering their buildings with grace and majesty.

In the cities, almost all the houses are roofed with tiles, which are very thick and semi-circular. Their convex side is placed downwards and further tiles are placed, the other way up, over the adjoining sides to cover the joins.

Chinese architecture makes great use of galleries, almost all of which are built to curious designs. These consist of pillars or open to one side by means of a series of windows of differing shapes. The galleries are used to link the main parts of buildings that are fairly distant from each other, sometimes with little gardens in between. The curious fact is that the arcades are rarely straight, but twist and turn, sometimes behind a bush, in front of a rock, sometimes encircling a little pool or mounting a little slope. Those built in front of apartments form eaves to protect the windows from the rains and the heat of the sun; these are all open and are called *lune-kane*.

Glass is not employed to glaze the windows; the common practice is to form the casements from thin paper stuck to a light trellis.

Above : the double roofs for which Chinese architecture is famous. Facing : a pavilion of the Forbidden City.

Doors, like the windows, may be of any shape: square, round, oval, shaped like fans, flowers, vases, birds, fish, etc. In the imperial palaces, the doors of the great apartments are doubled leafed and made up of solid wood up to a certain level, while the rest is open-work, depicting the outlines of flowers or animals or Chinese characters.

The stoves heating all the apartments are outside, in a sort of ditch into which the servant responsible for banking up the fires descends twice a day. All these charcoal-burning stoves are in the shape of a truncated cone and, through pipes winding and ramifying under the bricks (used instead of slabs to form the floors of apartments), they transmit a pleasant, moderate heat to the inside.

The Chinese liking for high towers has been a consistent theme of their history; in many provinces, there virtually is no town or even a village in which no such building exists. The design of these towers, however, normally follows the same pattern: it consists of hexagons or octagons divided into seven, eight and sometimes ten floors, decreasing gradually in size from the base to the tip. Each floor is delineated by a sort of cornice sustaining a six or eight leaf roof, from the corners of which hang little bells. Each floor is dominated by an encircling gallery with an ornate balustrade. This was the general plan used for the construction of the beautiful tower at Nankin, the most famous of all to be seen today in China and the most singular building in the whole of the East.

This tower was constructed 500 years ago and is called by the Chinese the *Temple of Gratitude;* it rises up from the middle of the numerous vast buildings of a bronze foundry situated outside the walls of the city.

The great number of rivers and canals which water China, especially its southern provinces, have made it necessary to build a prodigious quantity of bridges whose design varies greatly. Some are stilted, and stairs are provided to climb up one side and down the other; others have neither arches nor vaults but are built on large stones laid on piles like planks. Some of these stones are of extraordinary length. Many bridges are built of stone, marble or brick, while others are fashioned from wood or are pontoon bridges. The latter is a very ancient invention

66

they are known by the name of *seou-kiao,* floating bridges, and several are to be found on the large rivers.

Here we should mention the Great Wall of China, the famous wall extending for a distance of five hundred leagues, the length of three large provinces in the north—an eternal monument to the power of the Chinese and the most extraordinary structure ever executed by the hand of man. This marvel, which outshines all those of ancient Egypt, is all the more astonishing if we observe two points: the wall continues right up into the highest mountains and it is hard to conceive how this enormous boulevard could have been built at such great heights, especially in the dry and arid regions where it must have been necessary to transport water, bricks, cement and all the materials needed for the construction of this major work.

Another observation is that the wall is not straight but curves and winds at several places, sometimes following the line of the mountains, sometimes forming virtually a closed loop, so that it might be said that certain parts of China are defended by a triple wall, not just by one.

All historians are unanimous in naming the emperor Shih Huang Ti (246-210 B.C.) as being responsible for most of this magnificent structure.

The whole body of the wall is built of brick and it rests on a bed of wide, square stones. It is flanked with towers of differing shape and size. Some are merely a single storey high, the others have two floors and a terrace on the top with a parapet. These floors communicate with the platform of the wall by doors and stairways. The parapets of the towers and of the wall are provided with loop-holes. The distances between the towers are not constant but are closer in those places where it has been thought necessary to reinforce a given section of the wall. It is said that the Great Wall used once to be guarded by a million soldiers.

It is from the Chinese that the English acquired the taste for their simple gardens so close to nature.

A Jesuit, Fr. Cibot, and a Chinese author have told us of the ideal garden as seen in

Left: the Pagoda of the Thousand Bells (Peking). Below: a typical rural bridge (detail from early print).

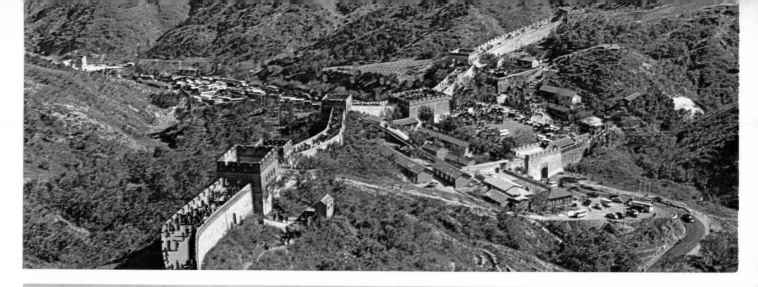
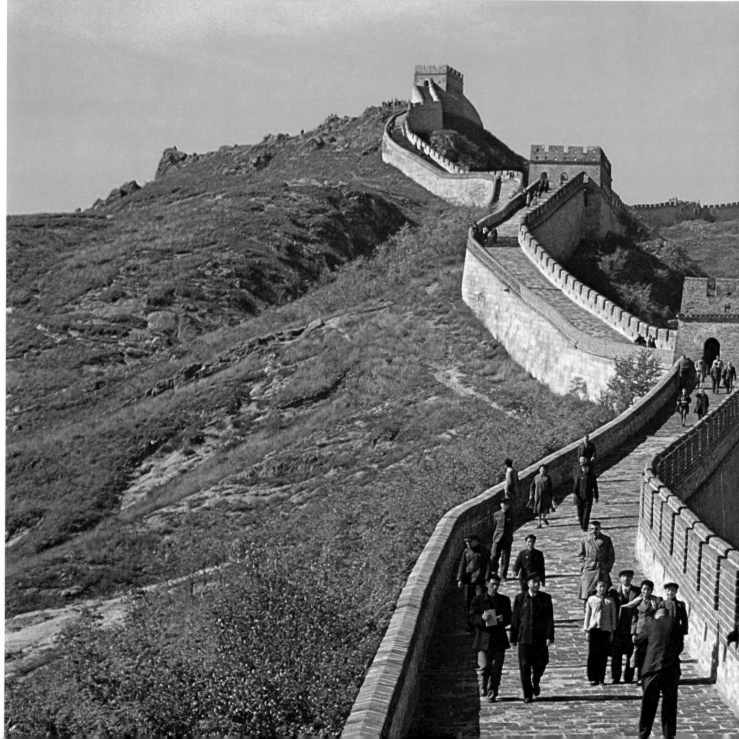

The Grest Wall, several views of which are shown here, is undoubtedly one of the most famous sights in China.

China, how to lay them out, and the different kinds of decoration used to adorn them. What should one seek, asks Lieou Chou, in a private pleasure garden, but a recompense for deprivation of the ever-agreeable sight of the countryside, the natural habitat of man? A garden must be a living and moving image of everything to be found in the country, producing in the soul the same feelings and providing the same joys for the eyes. The art of laying out a garden, therefore, consists of assembling in an equally unsophisticated way the greenness, shade, water, views, variety and solitude of the fields so that the eye is deceived by this imitation. Variety, the essence of the beauty of the countryside, is the first effect at which we should aim at when laying down the soil for a garden. If it is not large enough to provide all the aspects offered by nature, choose among them and arrange your choices in such a manner that, when combined, they bear the imprint of simplicity, negligence and caprice that renders so attractive and so delightful the sight of the countryside. A garden of taste is a place where the beauty of the spot, the pleasures of the situation and the variety of views are embellished by a carefully matched mixture of slopes, valleys and plains, running water and still water, small islands, bushes and isolated trees, grottos, peaceful open spots and wild solitude. To the extent possible, one should attempt to copy nature, trying to unite in a limited space what she has provided in the innumerable scenes and perspectives of the country.

In Chinese gardens, there is no alignment, no symmetrical relationships, for these are foreign to nature, which nowhere provides the spectacle of trees planted to form alleys, flowers collected together in beds or waters enclosed in regular polygons. The hills and little slopes are almost always clothed with different trees, planted in places close together as in a forest, sometimes by themselves or scattered here and there as in the fields. Their foliage, their freshness, their form, their volume and the height of their trunk: these are the factors that decide whether they will grow to the north or the south, on the top or on the side of the hills or in the gorges and passes formed by the hills.

A farm... A garden in bloom... The garden belonged to Emperor Yang, who had his palace surrounded by promenades entirely covered with peach and plum blossom. "In the middle of the park there was a lake which was itself surrounded by small houses inhabited by several hundred young girls whom the emperor used to invite to go riding on ponies in the moonlight or to glide along the lake on a boat, gently lulled by the night breeze."

After the Great Wall, the Avenue of the Tombs of the Ming emperors is the second major attraction in the vicinity of Peking. Here we see some of the animal statues along the avenue.

Other animal statues of the Avenue of the Mings. Right: the map of the avenue on a sign at the entrance. Note particularly the portico, which is reproduced on page 2, and the tombs, thirteen in number, of the emperors of the famous dynasty.

十三陵遊览示意图

	明 楼	4	石人石兽
1	石牌坊		
2	大宫门	5	龙凤门
3	碑 楼	6	七孔桥

An astonishing discovery which dates from only 1974; the three ditches of terra cotta statues of warriors and horses of Qin Shi Huand Di. While digging a tomb, the members of a people's commune found the beginning of eleven galleries paved with bricks, containing the statues arranged in combat formation, some of them in 38 rows. Excavations are continuing: it is estimated that the site contains some eight thousand statues... all of them life-size!

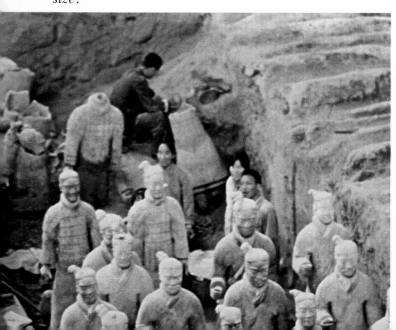

6

The *kin* or canonical books of the Chinese in all places advance the idea of a supreme Being, the creator and preserver of all things. They designate this Being by the names of *Tien,* or sky; *Chan-Tiene* or supreme sky; *Chan-ti,* supreme lord; *Hoan-Chan-ti,* sovereign and supreme lord. This sovereign being, say the books, is the originator of all that exists, the father of all men: he is eternal, unchanging, independent. His power is boundless, he can survey the past, present and future; he can see into the most intimate recesses of our hearts. He governs the sky and the earth; all the events, all human revolutions are the result of his provisions and his orders. He is pure, saintly, impartial. His eyes are offended by evil-doing and they rest with pleasure upon the virtuous deeds of man. Just and severe, he punishes vice even of those who sit upon the throne; at his will, he causes a guilty prince to fall and, if he so desires, he promotes to his place a man of obscure origins who may be to his heart. Good, clement, quick to forgive, he

allows himself to be moved by human repentance. Public calamities, the disorders of seasons are no more than salutary warnings given in his paternal goodness to his peoples so that they may mend their ways. These are the characteristics and attributes of the divinity as set out in almost every page of the *Chou-kin* and other canonical works.

Do heavy rains or long droughts threaten the harvest? Has a virtuous emperor, the father of this people, been struck by sickness? Sacrifices will be prepared immediately, solemn vows will be addressed to the *Tien.* Has an impious prince been laid low? This is not mere chance but the punishment is to be attributed to the visible justice of the *Tien.*

This doctrine on the existence and attributes of a sovereign being, on the cult and homage due to him, has persisted in China for many centuries. Were we to view all the monuments, to read all the canonical works of this nation, were we to consult the oldest of its annals, we would discover no trace of idolatry during reign after reign. Chinese history, so thorough in detail, so careful to report on all innovations, never mentions a superstitious rite that contravenes the belief and cult that we have attributed to the early Chinese. There is no doubt that historians would have recorded any such departure with the same scrupulous regard for truth with which they tell us of the establishment of the

Left : detail from a "rose family" vase with the "thousand flowers" motifs (Ts'ing period). Above : painted and gilded wooden statue of bodhisattva (7th century).

tao-se and the introduction of the absurd religion of the god *Fo,* an idol brought from India in later times.

The first sacrifices that the Chinese introduced in honour of the *Chan-ti* were offered in the open countryside or on the mountains, on a round pile of stones or a heap of earth.

Around this pile or « *tane* » was a double enclosure known as the "*kiao*", consisting of branches and turf. In the empty space between these two enclosures, at the right and left were raised two smaller altars on which, immediately following the sacrifice to the honour of the *Tien,* sacrifices were made to the *chene* and the *chen,* in other words to the higher spirits of all orders and to the virtuous ancestors. The sovereign, who was regarded as the "high priest" of the empire, was the only one to sacrifice on the "*tane*".

The most reliable commentators on the old books and all the writers who have discussed the doctrines of antiquity agree that this custom of making sacrifices to the *chene* and the *chen* after sacrificing to the *Chan-ti* dates back to the earliest times.

Since the emperors Yao and Chung, we have far more detailed information on these sacrifices. In the *Chou-kin* and other fragments of old history we read that Chung decreed:

1. That at the second moon, in which the equinox of spring took place, the sovereign would go to the Tai-chang mountain in the easternmost area of China and there he would sacrifice on a *tane* in the enclosure of a *kiao* to ask the Sky to deign to watch over the seeds that had been entrusted to the earth and were beginning to germinate;

2. That at the fifth moon, marking the summer solstice, the sovereign went to the southern mountain to perform the same ceremonies, asking the Sky for benign heat to be spread into the entrails of the earth to help it to develop all its virtues;

3. That at the eighth moon, which included the autumn equinox, a sacrifice was offered on the western mountain so that no insects or destructive animals, drought or over-humidity, wind or other forms of bad weather should prevent an abundant harvest of all the gifts that the soil produces for the use of man;

4. Finally, that in the twelfth month, after

the winter solstice, he would sacrifice on the northern mountain to thank the Sky for all the blessings received during the year and ask for further blessings during the year that was about to begin.

The custom of visiting these four mountains in turn persisted for many years. The emperors of the Chou dynasty added certain ceremonies and went to a fifth mountain situated in the middle of their states, or at least supposed to be between the four others; they then became known as the five

Yo or sacrificial mountains.

It was felt, however, that this institution, forcing the sovereign to make so many journeys, had its drawbacks. When the emperor had a capital, a court, and courts of justice established to expedite his business, it was difficult, even dangerous, for him to leave his place of residence at such regular intervals at the beginning of the four seasons. The arrangement made to overcome these drawbacks was to consecrate, near the palace, a place which could be used instead of the five *Yo,* in all circumstances, when the sovereign was unable to go to the true sacrificial mountains. A building was constructed there which was to represent both the *kiao* and the *tane.* The building consecrated to the practice of the religion was known by a different name

*Left: gilded bronze Buddha, of the T'ang period.
Above: the famous sage Lao-Tseu on his buffalo
(Musée Guimet, Paris).*

and took a new form under each of the first three dynasties.

Pekin has two main temples, the *Tiene-tane* and the *Ti-tane*. In the construction of these buildings, the Chinese deployed all their beauty and pomp of which their architects were capable. It is a matter of etiquette that no emperor may use equally rich or magnificent architecture for their palaces, and this rule extends to everything employed to decorate them, even the vases, utensils and musical instruments. Flutes, drums and other instruments producing music for the sacrifices are not only more exquisitely worked and more precious than those in the palace but are also made larger, so that it can truthfully be said that only in the *Tiene-tane* can great Chinese music be heard. The two temples are also dedicated to the *Chian-ti,* but on two different counts: one is the *temple of the eternal spirit,* while the other is devoted to adoration of the *spirit creating and conserving the world.*

Every year the emperor visits the Tiene-tane during the winter solstice to offer up a sacrifice to the Sky on a raised place, a round,

At the time of the Summer solstice the emperor is taken back to Ti-tan in order to offer up a sacrifice for the earth. Most scholars make a sharp distinction between the Ti-tan and the Tien-tan sacrifices, but in both cases the Supreme Being was the sole object of worship and both these cults were instituted primarily to honour the spirit which reigns over the universe, in accordance with the great and ancient doctrine.

These solemn sacrifices are offered up at the break of dawn. Before these important ceremonies are due to take place, the monarch, his courtiers, the mandarins and everyone who is entitled to assist them, all prepare themselves for the events to come by isolating themselves, fasting and by observing the rules of continence.

The Chinese character *chay,* which expresses this state of recollection, does not only mean abstinence and fasting but also, according to the Chinese dictionary, it designates in its most rigorous sense *denial of all things which could taint or corrupt the purity of the heart.*

The small amount of knowledge of physics and of natural phenomena has for a long time contributed to the success of superstitious beliefs in China and to facilitating the machinations of imposters. Half educated people, women and almost all of the lower classes have only to experience an unforeseen or unusual event to immediately attribute it to the hidden influence of some evil spirit. This spirit is created by each person in the delirium of his imagination; some associate it with a particular idol, others see it in an old oak tree, others again believe it to inhabit a high mountain or else the body of an enormous dragon living on the ocean bed. There is no end to the variety of sacrifices and strange ceremonies which have been invented to appease this evil spirit.

There are some who see this powerful enemy in another manner: according to them it is the soul, or rather the emanation or purified substance of an animal, such as a fox, a cat, a monkey, a tortoise or a frog. They assure us that when these animals have lived for some time they are then able to slough off the earthly part of their beings and so become pure spirit. This is when they are able to torment men and women alike, frustrate their plans and inflict fevers and all kinds of ills on them. In this case, when a person is confined to bed by one of these illnesses, the only doctor who can help them is the *tao-tze* who, when called in, fills the house with a deafening clanging and shouting to drive away the malignant spirit.

There are three more customs to be mentioned here. The first is called *suan-min,* the reading of the future. Every town in China is full of readers of horoscopes; these people are usually blind and go from house to house offering to tell the future events in exchange for a few coins. They adopt a special scientific jargon to make their predictions sound more impressive, and one cannot help but admire them for the vast variety of conclusions they can draw from the different combinations and positions of the astral bodies, not to mention all the details they can give on the year, the

Emperor Tang, clearly a Chinese relative of Saint Francis of Assisi. "Walking one day in the country, he saw some people who were catching birds with nets; he ordered them to set them free." His clemency is thought to have been the reason why thirty-six kings came to declare their allegiance to him.

month, the day and the exact moment of birth.

The second custom is to do with learning what one's fate is to be, and this can be done in a variety of ways. The commonest of them is to go to one of the idols, burn some incense before it and touch the ground several times with one's forehead. On the altar on which the idol stands, there is always a cornet-shaped receptacle filled with small flat sticks about six inches long, on which are inscribed various unintelligible characters. Each of these sticks contains an oracle. So when the prostrations and preliminary ceremonies have been completed, the person who would like to know what the oracles have in store for him lets one these little sticks fall to the ground at random, and then the bonze interprets the inscription on it for him. If no bonze is available the man can have the message deciphered by means of a card hanging on the wall. This way of discovering one's destiny is very frequent in China and there are a great many people who would think it most imprudent to embark upon a journey, engage upon buying or selling, or a court case, or contract a marriage without first consulting an oracle.

Fon-chui is another superstition of the Chinese and perhaps one of the most absurd of which human nature is capable. The word means *wind* and *water* and therefore the harmonious or ill-omened condition of a house, tomb or any other kind of building. If a man finds that next door to his house another thoughtless person has built one which does not follow the same architectural plan, if the new house has a roof which juts out and encroaches on the wall or the side of the old house, then this is considered a terrible disaster. The owner of the old house is seized by terror because he and all his descendants will be constantly under the evil influence of this threatening angle of the newly built roof. So the erection of the new building becomes the object of implacable enmity between the two families and often leads to lawsuits. If taking the matter to court cannot give any satisfaction, there remains only one way out to the offended house-owner, which is to place on the centre of his roof an enormous monster or dragon in baked clay. This monster has its fero-

cious glare fixed on the ill-omened angle of the roof, while its mouth is opened wide to swallow the sinister influence of the *fon-chui:* in this way a measure of safety can be obtained.

The name of Confucius is attached to or has connections with most of the institutions in China. We shall follow Western custom here by using this Latinised name for the famous philosopher who in his own country was known by the name of *Kung Fu-tse*. China who calls him *the holy master, the wisest sage,* proudly gives him the place of honour among the great men she has produced, and in fact no-one has attracted greater honours nor been the object of more universal veneration which has become almost a religion.

Confucius was born in the kingdom or state of Lu which today is part of the province of Shantung, in the year 551 B.C. in the small town of Tscu-y, today called Kin-fou-Hienne or Tscu-Hien, of which his father was governor, though he died when Confucius was only three years old. The little boy progressed rapidly in his studies, and his avoidance of all childish games, together with the great seriousness with which he approached everything he did, marked him out as a most exceptional child. Then he became a young man of exceptional wisdom, rivalling with the most learned scholars in his knowledge of ancient rites and customs.

At the age of seventeen Confucius made his entry into public service by exercising the duties of a junior mandarin; that is, he had to inspect the corn and other foodstuffs which were sold as basic commodities for the consumption of a large town. Then when he was nineteen his mother married him to the young Ki-koan-che, daughter of one of the oldest families in the empire, and the following year their first son, Pe-yu, was born. His exemplary behaviour and success

The determination of the astral signs and some of the trappings of "revelation" (Peking, Museum of the People). Following pages : landscape of the Ming period and picture of the town of Peking sculpted on an elephant's tusk.

in his first post, caused him to be promoted shortly afterwards to a more responsible position which involved the supervision of the surrounding countryside and its agricultural communities. Confucius carried out these functions for four years and was much loved by the people under his administration.

The death of his mother when he was twenty four, caused him to interrupt his administrative functions. The ancient Chinese laws which forbade the carrying out of any public functions for a certain period of time to all those who had lost one of their parents, had by now almost been forgotten, but Confucius, who strictly observed the old rites and customs and wanted to revive a respect for them in his own country, made a point of observing them. He wanted the last respects to be paid to his mother in exactly the same manner as in the old days, and when the amazed people in the town in which he lived saw and understood what he was doing, they also began to follow his example whenever they too were bereaved. So after this restoration of the old funeral rites, the entire nation continued to follow the custom for over two thousand years.

Once he had discharged these first duties towards his mother, Confucius shut himself up in his house to spend in solitude the three years of mourning. Then when this period was over he went to render his last homage to his mother by placing on her tomb his clothes of mourning, so that he was now free to wear his ordinary clothes again.

These three years of retreat were not wasted, because Confucius spent the time in deep philosophical study. He reflected for a long time on the eternal laws of morals,

This page : figure of Bodhisattva (Wei period). Right : two pictures of Confucius surrounded by his disciples.

followed them back to their sources, probed deeply into the duties and obligations they imposed on all men, and decided to make these moral laws the immutable rule governing all his actions. However, in order to be more sure of reaching this high state of virtue, he first applied all his concentration on discovering in the *Ching* (the Canons) and in historical writings, the different methods by which the ancient sages had attempted to reach a state of moral virtue.

Finally, when he had completed all these investigations, Confucius decided upon the way of life he should lead. At this time the Cheu dynasty was in power and was already sinking into decadence: licentiousness and ostentatious display reigned at Court, and there were constant wars. As this lack of discipline spread to the people, they too began to forget the ancient Canons of virtue. So Confucius decided to give up his quiet life, together with the fortune and honours

to which his high birth and considerable talents gave him the right, and dedicate himself to the modest life of teaching. His aim was to awaken in the minds of his fellow citizens a love and respect for the ancient Canons and customs from which he was sure that all social and political virtues emanated. Not only did he want to explain to his compatriots all the instructions and precepts which were an invariable part of moral order, but he also decided to open a school in which his disciples could be trained, so that they could help him to spread his doctrine over the whole empire and continue with the teaching even after his death. He even planned to write a series of books containing his maxims which extolled the ancient virtues which he so wished to inculcate into the minds of all his followers.

Every part of the plan was successfully carried out by this great Chinese philosopher. The mission to which he had dedicated his

90

life also caused him some bitterness and sorrow; people reacted to him in a number of contradictory ways, so that he might be welcomed in some royal courts while despised and almost a figure of fun in others. Towards the end of his life, exhausted by his long years of teaching, he was saddened that his work had only resulted in a very little sterile praise; he could not foresee the immense success it would have after his death, nor the long-lasting influence it would have on his country. No other philosopher or sage of those ancient times ever had the brilliant destiny that Confucius had, nor has anyone gathered such great honours, if only post-humously; never has the doctrine and teaching of one man had the honour of being incorporated into the legislation of a huge country, as was his. The moral teaching of Socrates has not changed the way of life of a single village in Attica, while the ethics of the great Chinese philosopher have governed the most vast and densely populated empire in the world for over two thousand years.

It was during one of his journeys that Confucius, together with some companions of his, had occasion to meet the famous Lao-tzu who was renowned everywhere for being a most extraordinary man whose conduct and doctrine was entirely different from anything seen or heard till then. This philosopher who had founded the Tao-tze sect of monks, was well used to being approached in his place of retreat by a great number of admirers and people of all ranks, so he received Confucius with some indifference. He was seated on a form of couch and made no move to greet him, he just deigned to lift his eyes and glance at these strangers whose names were announced to him and who had come, he was told, from very far

away to have the satisfaction of seeing him and hearing from his own mouth the doctrine he taught.

So Lao-Tzu looked at Confucius and said: "I have heard speak of you and I know you by reputation. I understand that you constantly speak of the ancients and that their maxims are always on your lips. But what is the use of taking so much trouble in trying to revive the ideas of men who ceased to exist so many years ago? The wise man should only concern himself with the period in which he lives and the circumstances of the present. If the moment and circumstances are favourable, he should act on them. If, on the contrary, this moment and these circumstances are unfavourable, he should withdraw and wait quietly without worrying about what other people are doing. If a man owns a great fortune, he is mindful not to tell all the world about it, he keeps it carefully so that he might use it should the need arise; if you are wise, you will do the same. Judging from your conduct, there seems to be much ostentation behind your plans to achieve wisdom, and you are inclined to be arrogant. Correct this fault in yourself, purge your heart of all love of pleasure; this will be much more useful to you than your attempts to learn about people who have long since died. You wanted to

Above: the temple of the Blue Clouds, Peking. Kneeling person at prayer. Right: Lohan, a disciple of the Buddha.

know what doctrine I teach: I have just given you a summary of it, so now act on it. I have nothing more to say to you".

Confucius was not at all offended at these stern words from the old man. He simply said to his disciples as he came away from the interview: "I have seen Lao-tzu, and now that I have seen him I know as little about him as I do about the dragon". It is very possible that Confucius did not want to comment at that moment on the character of a philosopher whose thought was so diametrically opposed to his own. Lao-tzu placed the greatest emphasis on the fact that an individual should concentrate on fulfilling himself and seeing to his own happiness, this was the essence of his doctrine. Confucius, on the other hand, wanted man to find the best way by which he could help his fellow beings.

The manner in which Confucius taught his pupils was very different from the methods used by the other teachers in schools where the time-table and syllabus were predetermined and unalterable. Confucius' pupils went to see him whenever they felt the necessity to do so and stayed as long as they wished. It was for them to decide upon the subject they wanted to learn, by asking for an explanation of various points in ethics, politics, history or literature. Confucius had over three thousand disciples, but one should not imagine that this number was made up of a huge crowd of young people gathering regularly around their master to gain knowledge under his discipline. These disciples who had received instruction from the great philosopher at different periods, were mostly men of mature years already engaged in various professions and trades, living with their families; they were scholars, mandarins, town governors and military men, living in all the states of the Chinese empire. Their affectionate attachment for their master led them to hurry to him every time their travels, or his, brought them together in the same part of the land. They prided themselves on professing his doctrine and spread his teaching in the areas in which they lived.

Among these pupils there was, however, a small group of people especially keen on the study of philosophy who were strongly attached to their master; they lived with him, saw to all his needs and followed him almost everywhere he went.

Confucius had been enjoying the rest and satisfactions of private life for some years, when suddenly the king of Lu died. The new emperor did not share his predecessor's indifference for this philosopher who was a subject of his and who was already renowned all over the empire for his teaching. The new emperor hoped to be able to gain from the virtues and talents of this highly esteemed and wise old man, so he summoned him to his court where he welcomed him warmly, then they had a long conversation at the end of which the emperor decided to make Confucius his closest confidant. Soon the philosopher was put in positions of higher and higher authority over the people and he became governor, then supreme judge at the courts of justice and finally was made minister. The energy, courage and impartiality which Confucius showed in the exercise of these duties were truly exceptional and brought him even greater fame.

This fame and success began to worry the king of Tsi whose territories were adjacent to those of Lu and who had just gained possession of his throne by murdering the previous king. So the king of Tsi resolved to entirely undo the good work of Confucius by means of a clever plan. He knew that the king of Lu had a frivolous nature and a great taste for the pleasures of life, so under the pretext of renewing diplomatic relations between the two kingdoms he appointed an ambassador to visit the young sovereign and bring him some presents. Now these gifts were of great magnificence but of a very novel kind and extremely treacherous in their attractiveness. They consisted of thirty highly trained horses, a great quantity of jewels and rare objects, and last, but not least, eighty beautiful girls some of whom were talented in music, others in dancing and others again were good actresses.

Top right : scene from the life of Confucius. He is distributing to poor peasants a thousand measures of rice donated by a minister, whose apparent generosity is in fact motivated by ostentation and vanity. Bottom : statuette of the sage Li-Tai-Po.

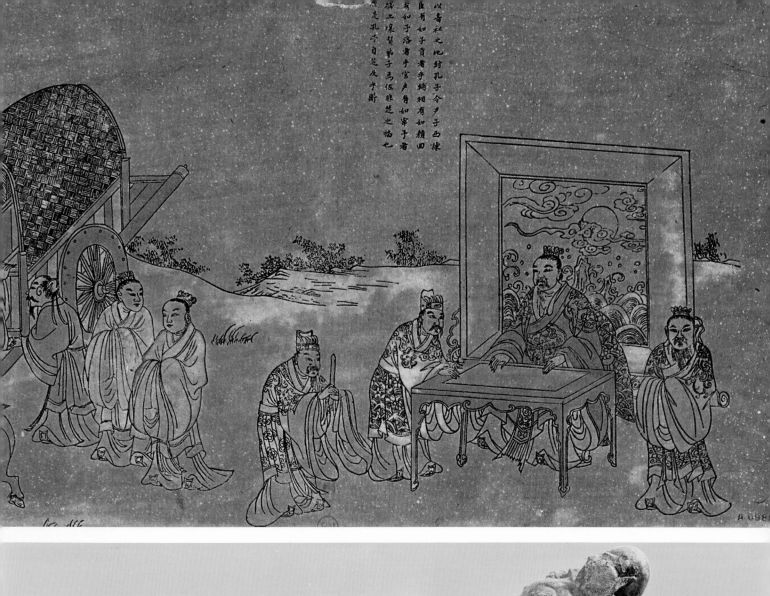

以善祀之地封孔子令夕子西諫
曰有如子貢者于朝相有如顏四
有如子路者于官戶身有如宰予者
使工堰賢弟子為佐非楚之福也
是孔子自楚反中衛

How could any philosophical system compete against such a bevy of young and sprightly beauties intent on pleasing and armed with all possible means of seduction? It did not take long for the sombre and austere life of the court to capitulate to the good-natured follies of the beautiful foreigners, so that no-one thought of anything other than parties, theatrical entertainments, dances and concerts. In vain Confucius tried to deter the people from their reckless life by reminding them of the laws and moral precepts; no-one listened to him. Even the king who was as intoxicated with his pleasures as was the rest of the court, became tired of the constant admonishments of his philosopher-adviser and banished him from his presence.

So Confucius, now in disgrace, left his country to lead a life of retirement in the company of his disciples, choosing to live in the kingdom of Uei where he stayed for over ten years without ever seeking public office, but instead he concentrated on writing further books, instructing his disciples and spreading his doctrines. However, he did make several journeys to the other states in the empire. Sometimes he was sought after and applauded, but more often he suffered considerable persecution and was even in danger of being killed on more than one occasion. He experienced great poverty, hunger and

often had nowhere to live or take shelter. He once likened himself to a dog which had been driven away from its home: "I am as faithful as this animal", he said, "and I am treated just like a dog. But what does the ingratitude of man matter to me? This will not stop me from doing as much good as I can, so even if my teaching has no effect I shall at least have the consolation of knowing that I have done my duty".

At last, at the age of 68, Confucius was able to return to his country after fourteen years of absence. Now he lived as a private citizen and was occupied with putting the final touches to his collections of writings.

In his seventy third year, after a serious illness, he fell into a deep coma from which all the efforts of medical science could not awaken him, and so he died in the year 479 B.C., nine years before the birth of Socrates.

When the old philosopher died, all his disciples were gathered around him, and at his funeral one of them planted a *kiai* tree on his grave. This extraordinarily long-lasting tree which is now just a dried-out trunk with no branches, can still be seen in the same spot in spite of all the upheavals of twenty three centuries; it has become a venerable monument for the Chinese who have had their artists draw it with the greatest care and then engrave their picture on a piece of marble, from which innumerable prints were made to adorn the rooms of most of the scholars in that country.

The custom of hanging a portrait of Confucius in the state schools began in the year 179 A.D. Then statues were made instead of portraits; the first of these appeared at the beginning of the Tan dynasty and were made in wood and clay, carefully painted to give them a realistic appearance. In 1457 Yn-tson, eight emperor of Min, had a statue of Confucius cast in brass which was to stand in one of the rooms of his palace, then he ordered that "each time his ministers came to the palace they should first enter this room to pay their respects to Kung Fu-tse before speaking to him or to each other of affairs of state".

After a while, there came to be so many statues and portraits of Confucius as to provoke the protests and disapproval of the

austere upholders of the plain life of ancient times. So in 1530 the emperor ordered their suppression and replaced them with tablets inscribed with the names of Confucius or those of his disciples. It was decided that the inscription should read as follows: *Tche-chen-sien-che Kung Fu-tse*, which means *Kung Fu-tse, the wisest sage, the great and ancient master*. The tablet for Yen-tse, his favourite disciple, bears these two words: *fu-chen*, which mean *the second wisest man*.

Contrary to what some writers have believed, Confucius never had any legislative power in China, he was never invested with such authority as to be able to lay down new laws, and at no time did he consider making changes in the religion of his country. Like Socrates who came after him he concerned himself with ethics. Far from inventing his precepts, he constantly referred to himself as a transmitter—not the originator—of maxims taught by his ancient predecessors.

Confucius is held to be not only the greatest and most profound philosopher in his country, but also its best writer.

Left: the god of happiness. Facing: ivory statue of a sage (3th century BC). Below: the Temple of the Lama, Peking. Last page: statuette of a mounted hunter (T'ang period).